EDGE
of the
SACRED

Transformation in Australia

D0707007

David J. Tacey

HarperCollins*Publishers*

Published by HarperCollins*Publishers* (Australia) Pty Ltd
(ACN 008 431 730)
22–24 Joseph Street
North Blackburn, Victoria 3130, Australia

First published 1995
Reprinted 1995
Designed by William Hung
Cover design by William Hung
Cover photo of Mt Ebenezer sand dunes, Northern Territory;
courtesy of Coo-ee Picture Library, Melbourne

Typeset by HarperCollins*Publishers*, Melbourne
Printed in Australia by Griffin Paperbacks

The National Library of Australia
Cataloguing-in-Publication data:

Tacey, David J. (David John), 1953–   .
  Edge of the sacred : transformation in Australia.

  Includes index.
  ISBN 1 86371 408 1.

  1. Jung, C.G. (Carl Gustav), 1875–1961 — Religion.
  2. Psychology and religion. 3. Aborigines, Australian —
  Religion. 4. Religion and geography. 5. Australian
  Literature. 6. Australia — Religion — 20th century.
  I. Title.

291

Acknowledgements
Our thanks go to those who have given us permission to reproduce
copyright material in this book. Particular sources of print material
are acknowledged in the text.

Every effort has been made to contact the copyright holders of text
material. The author and publisher apologise in those cases where
this has proved impossible.

Excerpts from the work of D.H. Lawrence throughout this book
are reproduced with the permission of Laurence Pollinger Ltd
and the Estate of Frieda Lawrence Ravagli.

Extract on p. 138 from 'We are Going' by Oodgeroo of the tribe
Noonuccal (formerly Kath Walker), is reproduced with the permission
of Jacaranda Press.

to the memory of my grandfather
George Joseph Cain
1896–1989

Anzac, postman and mystic;
in gratitude for bringing sacred resonances
to ordinary life

What we have received
is the ordinary mail of the otherworld, wholly common,
not postmarked divine

— LES MURRAY[1]

Contents

of the dead; the woman who unmakes men; the
contrary impulse: desert mutilation versus city
barricades; last rites: keeping endless tryst.

RE-ENCHANTMENT

Preface

This is a generalist book on the psychological and spiritual situation of Australian society, written for a broad audience. Although I am a professional academic, and much of what I teach and write is 'in-house', I am not personally committed to a narrowly academic approach, but frequently attempt to address a wide range of issues from a generalist perspective. Having said that, I do not think it is sufficiently realised that academics in mass-institutions such as my own La Trobe University are directly involved in informed, generalist dialogue with the community on a daily basis. Only at senior levels of teaching are intellectual dialogues conducted for the very few in a specialist language. A large part of university teaching consists not in displaying professional wares, but in exploring topics with adults of varying ages and experience, of vastly different cultural and racial backgrounds, and of widely disparate intellectual interests and pursuits.

Educational activity in the broader public domain, including seminars and short courses for diverse groups of people, as well as involvement on radio and in newspapers, has taught me to eschew a single 'discipline' for a sense of intellectual responsibility to society as a whole. As a Jungian, this broad and cross-disciplinary approach is made easier by the fact that the theory of archetypes and of unconscious process knows no disciplinary boundaries, since by definition archetypal patterns are found everywhere and are discovered in every corner of human activity and enterprise. Although trained in literary study, I cannot confine my interest to novels and poems when archetypal patterns wink at me from other fields, from my own personal experience, and from sociopolitical life. 'English' itself has changed vastly from what it once was, and today concerns itself with the study of a very wide range of texts, cultures, and intellectual ideas. Nothing is definite, everything is problematical and questioned in the postmodern university.

The exploration of an Australian spirituality is a relatively recent cultural preoccupation, although the broader search for Australian identity has been vigorously conducted for at least a hundred and fifty years. Arguably, Manning Clark's monumental *History of Australia* attempted to discover (some would say 'impose') mythic and spiritual patterns in our national experience.[1] More recently, Les Murray has been engaged in an ongoing quest for an Australian spiritual identity, and his output and findings have been singularly impressive.[2] Tony Kelly's *A New Imagining: Towards an Australian Spirituality* and Veronica Brady's *Caught in the Draught* are highly suggestive and illuminating attempts to establish a religious framework for Australian cultural experience.[3] In the Foreword to Tony Kelly's book, Bishop Cuskelly writes: 'For several years now ... we have had the strong feeling that Australia might—very seriously—be in search of its soul. We who are Christian have dared to hope that this search would be conducted in the light of the Gospel'. Broadly speaking, all attempts so far to map the Australian soul have been conducted in light of Christianity, and mainly from a Roman Catholic perspective.

This book is the first to explore these issues from a Jungian perspective. The Jungian view is not compelled to discover a national soul that mirrors and confirms the tenets of Christian faith. While certainly not anti-Christian in its direction, Jungian psychology assumes from the outset that much that resides within the human soul is not Christian in its origin or structure. Since our collective consciousness is governed by Christian values and principles, Jungian thought would argue that, virtually by definition, what lies in the deep unconscious psyche (soul) is antagonistic to—or at best compensatory to—the structures of consciousness. St Augustine said that the soul is naturally Christian, but large parts of the modern soul are anything but.

My own grandfather, an Irish-Australian gnostic and rebel, taught me to believe that the Christian Church did not have a monopoly on the sacred.[4] I have come to accept this view as an a priori given in my own work and thought. However, the view that spirituality and the Church are antithetical is an extreme and radical view, which I am increasingly beginning to feel has no real foundation. Anti-Christianism has been a potent force in my development, first from my grandfather, then from my secondary and tertiary education (where we are taught that God is an infantile illusion), and again from my post-doctoral fellowship in the United States, which was conducted under the supervision of the Jewish scholar and post-Jungian analyst James Hillman. It has always struck me as ironic that, in what we complacently call a 'Christian country', the Christian viewpoint is consistently under attack and often undermined altogether.

The images we impose upon the character of the divine are inevitably 'man-made', and I am not about to involve myself in sectarian wars or political conflicts about which, or whose, image of the divine is closest to the truth. I am gradually outgrowing the anti-Christianism of my earlier years, and I am more interested today in how Christianity itself is undergoing transformation, as a result of our new and challenging experiences of the sacred. Here again I come back to Jung, who felt that the Western religious life was in a state of continuing change and self-revelation. Jung believed that the old image of God—the one attacked by Nietzsche and debunked by Freud—had indeed 'died' to Western culture, but that a new image of God would be born in our midst, an image that would fulfil contemporary human needs and at the same time reveal a new and previously undisclosed or 'unconscious' side of the Godhead. What excites me is the role that Australian experience can play in this archetypal drama of the death and rebirth of the sacred. The important task is to dream onward the interior life of the heart and the spirit, to relate this interior life to outward social change, and to continually attempt to build an intermediate realm of culture where inner and outer worlds can meaningfully relate to each other.

My work will not satisfy purists of any persuasion. My gnosticism is tempered by Christianity, my scholarship is coloured by speculation and intuition, and my Jungianism is modified by Freudian influence. Freud and some post-Freudians, Alfred Adler, Nietzsche and Hillman have added to, or detracted from, the direct and powerful influence of Jung. Studies in the Jungian mode often tend toward esotericism and withdrawal from the world in pursuit of spiritual enlightenment. My own work shares some of these traits, but I am frequently held back from interiority by a passionate concern for the social and political problems of contemporary society. I suppose that I subvert the conventional dualism of inner and outer reality by referring to an entity called 'the Australian psyche', which is an intermediate realm between interiority and society; a kind of collective interiority or imaginal place. Journalists often talk about the national psyche because it is a convenient fiction that allows them to make generalisations one step removed from statistical reality. For me the idea of a national psyche is an enabling device, a way of integrating apparently disparate materials, a notion that enables me to bring together the subtle concerns of the spirit with the raw facts of social experience.

❖   ❖   ❖

This book has been in preparation for some time. The idea first came to me in 1982 when I was working at the Dallas Institute of Humanities with James Hillman. Since, in the analytical side of our work, we were involved in the study of my dreams, Hillman was amazed at the amount of Australia that I carried around with me. As an American with no cause to find out much about us before, he was fascinated by the bits of history, social process, and political life that came up in my dreams. Analytical sessions would sometimes turn into history and geography discussions, and always we kept an eye out for the dominant Australian symbols and archetypal images. Captain James Cook appeared, but this time slaughtered by the Aboriginals; there were countless references to Alice Springs and Uluru, to camels, trains, distant horizons ('Just like Texas'); to Australian Rules Football; to Patrick White ('Yes, him again'); to gold, Ballarat, and the study of stones, dirt, and rocky ground. It was not until I had spent two years in the United States that the Australianness of my life and psyche became very clear to me—an experience often had by those who live and work overseas.

I would like to thank James Hillman, Patricia Berry, Tom Moore and Robert Sardello for providing me with a context for this book to bubble up for the first time. Tom Moore's weekly dream groups were wonderful opportunities to explore the mythic depths and resonances of cultural and social images. At the City University of New York, my thinking was helped very much by Harold Schechter, and at the University of Colorado by Martin Bickman. Numerous conversations with individual writers and scholars in other countries have furthered my understanding of the area of 'national psychology': these include Andrew Samuels in England (who is ambivalent about national psychology),[5] Ellen O'Malley in Ireland, Ralph Maud in Canada, Michael Harlow in New Zealand, and Sven Doehner and Patricia Ortega in Mexico.

I wish to acknowledge a major debt to my maternal grandfather, George Joseph Cain. George Cain conceived in Derry, Ireland, and born on the goldfields of Ballarat, Victoria. His entire life was a night-sea voyage of the spirit, and he explored, and shared with me, spiritualism, theosophy, Rosicrucianism, and Eastern philosophy. He was a World War veteran who survived the Gallipoli campaign, and his missing fingers reminded me continually of sacrifice. His thirst for spiritual mystery and transformation was matched only by his commitment to political change. He lived, like so many of his Irish forbears, simultaneously in secular and sacred reality, and he taught me to live in and value both the political and the spiritual world.

I am indebted to Molly Scrymgour, who first introduced me to Jung and the Jungian tradition, and who provided the 'psychological' turn to my developing spiritual interests. Peter Bishop in Adelaide has given me ongoing support and critical feedback.[6] My wife Sharon Gregory has shared numerous insights about Australia and her own indigenous Maori culture, and my six-year-old daughter Ana Rose Gregory-Tacey has put me in touch again with my own dreaming soul and the animated universe. Numerous individual scholars and persons have contributed to this work by conversation, by critical comment, or by making remarks that have informed my thinking. These individuals include Ian Austen, David Bathgate, Jim Bowler, Margaret Cain, John Carroll, Glenda Cloughley, Patricia Dutton, Susan Dwyer, Robert Farrell, Peter Fullerton, Rodney Hall, Paul Holman, Robert Hoskin, Diana James, Michael

Leunig, Brendan McPhillips, Roman Mankowski, Freya
Mathews, Gerald Murnane, Les Murray, Bernie Neville,
Peter O'Connor, William Ricketts, Val Rogers, Peter Ross,
Craig San Roque, Fran Sarell, Ross White. I am grateful for
the stimulation provided in formal and informal contacts
with these people.

I wish to acknowledge assistance from the La Trobe
University Outside Studies Programme, for making
available study leave and funds to enable me to bring this
book to completion. Assistance was also provided by the La
Trobe Centre for Archetypal Studies, which provided a
travel grant to attend a European symposium on archetypal
psychology in 1993. I would like to thank the members of
the School of English at La Trobe, and in particular its
recent heads, Lucy Frost and Richard Freadman, for
providing an encouraging intellectual environment and for
enabling me to teach courses on Jung and Hillman in the
School's programmes. Robin Freeman, Dianne Milwright
and Helen Pace of HarperCollins*Publishers* in Melbourne
have been most helpful from the beginning, and I wish to
record my thanks.

A number of these chapters were originally composed in
response to invitations to speak at conferences, symposia,
and other gatherings. I gratefully record the opportunity to
speak at a 1988 soirée at the house of Paul and Marta
Brown, which formed the basis for Chapter 1 of this book.
I thank Douglas Kirsner for inviting me to speak at the
Deakin University Freud Conference of 1991, from which
Chapters 2 and 3 originated. Chapter 4 was presented to the
Canberra Jung Society in 1992, Chapter 8 to the Bendigo
Jung Society in 1991, and the ideas in Chapter 6 were
originally developed for Mark Sumner's Melbourne
conference on Jung and Spirituality in 1992. The
Introduction was first presented as a talk for the La Trobe
1994 'Psyche in the World' conference.

During the process of writing, I submitted sections of this book for publication in international journals of Jungian thought and in Australian periodicals of literary and cultural studies. These appeared as follows:

An earlier version of Chapter 1 was published as 'At the Edge of the Sacred: Landscape and Dreaming', *Harvest: Journal for Jungian Studies* (London), Volume 40, November 1994, pp. 60–76.

Chapter 2 appeared as 'Descent into the Unconscious', *Island* (Hobart), Issue 55, Winter 1993, pp. 56–60; an American version was published as 'The Australian Psyche: Archetypal Process Down Under', *Psychological Perspectives* (Los Angeles), Issue 28, November 1993, pp. 32–43.

Chapter 3 was published as 'Dissolving into Landscape', *Island* (Hobart), Issue 56, Spring 1993, pp. 45–9; the American version was 'Falling Down to Earth: Psyche, Earth, and Sacrifice', *Psychological Perspectives* (Los Angeles), Issue 29, June 1994, pp. 104–15.

Chapter 4 appeared as 'On Not Crossing the Gap: D.H. Lawrence and Australia's *Genius Loci*', *Quadrant* (Melbourne), Vol. 34, No. 11, November 1990, pp. 69–73, and was reprinted as 'Australian Landscape as a Spiritual Problem', *Transforming Art* (Sydney), Vol. 4, No. 1, September 1992, pp. 15–21.

An earlier, longer version of Chapter 5 was published in my book *Patrick White: Fiction and the Unconscious*, Oxford University Press, 1988, pp. 69–90.

Parts of Chapters 7 and 8 were published as 'Australia's Otherworld: Aboriginality, Landscape, and the Imagination', *Meridian* (Melbourne), Vol. 8, No. 1, May 1989, pp. 57–65.

Two further sections of Chapter 8 were published as 'Dreaming Our Myths Onward', *Island* (Hobart), Issue 53, Summer 1992, pp. 58–62; and as 'Jung's Ambivalence Toward the World Soul', *Sphinx: A Journal for Archetypal*

Psychology and the Arts (London), No. 5, May 1993, pp. 278–87.

Parts of Chapter 9 appeared as 'Contemporary Spiritual Experience', *Vision* (Melbourne), Vol. 1, No. 1, Winter 1992, pp. 4–6.

I am extremely grateful to the editors of these Australian, English, and American journals for publishing this work, and for their careful editing of it, which has been incorporated in the present book.

D.J.T.

Helen Garner: 'Why are Australians so embarrassed about soul and … religion?'
Michael Leunig: 'About everything, so why not religion?'[1]

By *soul* I mean a perspective rather than a substance, a viewpoint toward things rather than a thing itself.
— JAMES HILLMAN[2]

No one has changed a great nation without appealing to its soul.
— ROBERT BELLAH[3]

Neither science nor politics can overcome the problems we face. What we need rather is a renewal of imagination, a transformation of the way we see the world.
— VERONICA BRADY[4]

I have a feeling in my bones that there is a possibility of a creative religious explosion occurring early in the next millennium with the ancient land of Australia at the centre of it.
— MAX CHARLESWORTH[5]

Introduction

➤

Recovering the
sacred in Australia

We have gills for dream-life, in our head; we must
keep them wet.

— LES MURRAY[1]

This book strives to present new images of the sacred in
that most secular of places: contemporary Australian
society. The desperate need in every secular society is to 'remake' the sacred, in the sense of *restoring our relationship*
to the sacred. This is a supreme art or craft: the ability to
track down the sacred, to revive and restore it, without
falling into religious literalism, fundamentalism, or
dogmatic thinking. Jungian psychology constructs the
sacred as a kind of autonomous complex in the modern
psyche, and it finds or recovers the sacred first of all in
psychopathology, in illness and neurosis, in the distortions
and obsessions of our contemporary behaviour. 'The
Gods have become diseases' wrote Jung,[2] and this large
theme is discussed at length in Chapter 9, 'Tracking the
Sacred in Secular Society'. Only by remaking and restoring
the sacred can we achieve individual and collective health,
since the sacred stands at the very heart of humanity, and
if it is repressed or ignored humanity must suffer the
consequences.

The call for resacralisation—a word I have borrowed
from Andrew Samuels[3]—is sometimes seen as eccentric or
inappropriate. Some religious colleagues argue that

*re*sacralisation is not necessary, since we already have access to genuine spiritual mysteries as these are embodied in the great religious traditions. However, with due respect to those who have been able to maintain their inherited faith, ours is a thoroughly secular age, which has experienced a widespread *disenchantment* and loss of religious perspective. The vast majority of educated, contemporary people have, like myself, experienced Nietzsche's 'death of God' and we are unable to pretend that the intellectual enlightenment, modernism, and now postmodernism, have not taken place. The opposite objection is raised by certain secular colleagues: why call for resacralising at all, when we have struggled so long and hard to achieve cultural freedom and liberation from archaic superstition? What sort of right-wing or reactionary 'agenda' do I have? Some people think it is crazy to attempt to bring back God just when we thought—or hoped—we had killed God off.

My own view is that this 'progressive' longing for freedom from the nonrational is inherently flawed and wrong-headed; it is out of date and certainly out of touch with the real spiritual needs of our time. The rationalist enlightenment did serve a purpose in the past: it freed us from the burdens and encumbrances of medievalism; it helped us break from a deterministic world-view that disempowered the individual and deprived men and women of intellectual, moral, and spiritual autonomy. But we have gone far enough down this road of freedom, and anyhow the prospect of liberation that it seemed to offer has proved to be illusory. A world-view based on the human element alone lands us squarely in the prison of the rational ego, where soul and spirit are banned, repressed, and ignored. Ironically, our secular 'humanism' has made us less than human, because a large part of the mystery of being human includes the needs and desires of that within which is *other* than human, that inside us which is archetypal, nonrational, and religious.[4] A 'post-rationalist' and truly postmodern enlightenment must involve a fuller wisdom and a broader grasp of human experience. It must recognise the paradoxical nature of human reality and understand that humanity and the sacred are reciprocal and interdependent entities: they make and remake each other.

The next step in our cultural evolution will involve, paradoxically, a step back from the rational intellect toward our culturally abandoned intuitive and wisdom faculty. Instead of feeling superior to those in the past who possessed faith and belief in the supra-human, we will need to follow their example to a large extent, because we have lost the art of intuitive perception; we no longer know or remember how to experience, feel, or recognise that which is other than human. As Jung and Lawrence knew, the way ahead is the way back, but this way back cannot be merely a regressive return to the past, but a recovery, in entirely new ways, of what has been lost. We need to develop not pre-modern mysticism but a *postmodern spirituality*,[5] one that meets the demands of the present in ways that are entirely in accordance with our advanced technical, scientific, and intellectual development. The new physics and the new biology are already moving toward a genuinely postmodern spirituality, and have been doing so for several decades.

Many Australians like to imagine that they inhabit a period of history that transcends the idea of the sacred: the influential editor of the Sydney *Bulletin* wrote in 1899, 'the religious stage was one stage in human evolution, as natural as the irreligious stage which is superseding it'.[6] An important perspective is offered by Mircea Eliade, who argues that the sacred is not a stage of human history that we have outgrown, but a crucial part of human experience that we have misunderstood by attempting to interpret it literally.[7] Of course, the *forms* of the sacred must change through time, but Eliade insists that the idea that we have outgrown the sacred in any form is a contemporary fallacy of colossal magnitude. Contemporary scientific rationalism has led to a religious cul-de-sac, where the symbolic statements of the soul are read literally as 'outdated misinformation' or primitive science about the nature of the real world. Anthropologists try hard not to denigrate the beliefs of archaic peoples, but they see those beliefs as fulfilling a merely social or structural function, as constructs that hold the society together, and not as an authentic means of maintaining and strengthening the bond between the human and the divine. Eliade and Jung have said that no high culture has ever attempted to live without a meaningful relation to the sacred, none has considered that the material level was an adequate basis for sustaining a healthy and coherent society. Eliade calls for a 'new humanism' that is not based on rational materialism, but assumes that the sacred is a basic category of human experience, and sees that the human cannot be separated from the nonhuman and the archetypal. According to Eliade, humanity is and will always remain *homo religiosus*, and human nature can only know and fulfil itself in relationship to a transcendent other.[8]

Australia as a natural site for recovering the sacred

Despite the fact that Australia appears to be one of the most secular and godless societies in the modern world, there is good reason to suppose that an authentic rediscovery of the sacred is already in preparation here. Although at an external level Australia seems committed to the heroic, rationalistic and ego-building values of Western culture, unconsciously there is a movement in the opposite direction, a tendency toward dissolving the ego and embracing the archetypal and elemental realm. I believe there is an *unconscious compulsion toward sacrifice* in the

Australian psyche, a compulsion that is difficult to explain rationally, but which is explored in Chapters 2 to 5 of this book. As discussed in 'The Need for Sacrifice' (Chapter 3), the sacrificial momentum derives from an intensification of the unconscious elemental psyche, which draws to itself contents and energies that otherwise would be available to the ego and used in the ego's service. This partial defeat or retardation of the ego can lead to a strengthening of the claims of the sacred other. Australians, by virtue of their historical and geographical conditions, are close to primordial reality almost by default.

However, if the ego loses too much ground to the unconscious, this can lead to its absorption into the archetypal sphere, in which case 'the sacred' becomes a devouring maw, which overwhelms and disintegrates humanity. Joan Lindsay's *Picnic at Hanging Rock*, Lawrence's *Kangaroo*, and Patrick White's *Voss* are powerful novels, which show this process at work in the Australian psyche, and these texts are explored in Chapters 3, 4, and 5 respectively. A negative mysticism or life-negating spirituality can readily develop when society is fragile, nascent, or too exposed to the overwhelming powers of the unconscious. As a counter-reaction to this weakening of the ego, society develops certain artificial forms of ego-strengthening. Australian society is notorious for its brute masculinity, its tough machismo, its laconic shyness, its disregard for the interior world and its disrespect for the nonrational. These traits are revealed in this book as strong defences, a 'masculine protest', against an unconscious psyche that, despite all appearances, has managed to win the upper hand.

At the present time many Australians are beginning to shed the psychological armour that society has built around us. This armour has served a purpose and it is not my wish to berate it entirely: it has stopped us from dissolving into the unconscious. It is too easy for people of my own generation to undermine the white pioneers and laugh at the way they created a psychological fortress in this unfamiliar land. But now that the usefulness of this fortress has passed, it is appropriate that we allow it to fall into disrepair and face the new challenges before us. We must now respectfully throw off the secular iron mask and move to a new level of development where much more of the world is embraced and integrated into consciousness. We have been living half-lives, or less, inside the cocoon of our social conditioning. The sacred lies in wait for our approach and is always accessible to those of us who drop the defences. If the human ego can learn to live in the presence of the sacred without being overwhelmed by it, then a genuine spirituality can emerge from the creative interaction of humanity and the sacred. This is the archetypal background that could readily result in Australia becoming a major site for the spiritual renewal and re-invigoration of the contemporary world.

Landscape as a key player in the Australian psyche

In Australia, landscape carries our experience of the sacred other. For two hundred years the majority of Australians have shielded themselves against the land, huddling together in European cities, pretending we are not in or part of Australia. But the landscape obtrudes, and often insinuates itself against our very will, as so much Australian writing testifies. The landscape in Australia is a mysteriously charged and magnificently alive archetypal presence. As Judith Wright has put it: 'In Australian writing the landscape seems to have its own life. Sometimes it takes up an immense amount of room; sometimes it is so firmly pushed away that its very absence haunts us as uncomfortably as its presence could'.[9] Although experienced by some as dull, flat, and uneventful, the

Australian landscape is in fact a most exciting archetypal field. The land is, or seems to be, the sacred which bursts in upon our lives, which demands to be recognised and valued. As George Johnston wrote, 'nothing human has yet happened in Australia which stands out above the continent itself'.[10]

This book is in large part about landscape and differing experiences of landscape. Australians can huddle in enormous coastal cities and pretend that the vast landscape is not there. Or we can impose human images and values upon the land, and imagine it as a friendly extension of the ego's world; a folksy playing field we call 'the Bush'. But the writings of White, Stow, Lindsay, Lawrence, and others show that the friendly pastoral patch, which nationalist sentiment referred to as 'the Bush', was never anything more than a temporary construct of the political imagination. The 'mournful genius of the plain', which had been 'driv'n from his primal solitary reign',[11] returned with a vengeance in the literature, painting, and music of the mid-twentieth century.

No matter how we attempt to package or construct it, the land will always break out of whatever fancy dress we foist upon it. The Australian landscape is our greatest asset, our assurance that any society here cannot afford to become complacent, that the other around us cannot be ignored or deprived of its shocking revelatory and transformative power. The only way to develop a spiritually powerful culture in Australia is to enter more into the psychic field of nature; to 'shamanise' ourselves in the image of nature. This is the subject of Chapter 8, 'Toward a New Dreaming'. We need to become less human and more like nature: in that way we may become more fully human, and experience anew the sacred fount from which all life, including our human life, arises.

The degraded sacred in white and black society

Drunk, he becomes more Australian ...
— Christopher Koch[12]

What has concerned me for a number of years is the way in which a split between the spiritual and the secular in Australian experience has manifested along racial lines. White Australians are often constructed as brazenly and gloriously secular, full of disbelief, cynicism, and blasphemy. Black Aboriginal Australians are frequently depicted as possessing sacred values, truths, and visions, and as inhabiting sacred space. This is understandable given the fact that the Aboriginal Dreaming is possibly the most ancient continuous sacred tradition on earth. But this convenient polarisation or splitting within the Australian psyche is very costly indeed. By virtue of this split, white Australians are denied access to sacredness (especially the sacredness of the land), and black Australians, often imprisoned in the 'religious' category, are denied access to materiality, wealth, and economic security. The split is convenient, but it is also fatal, and this will be further explored in Chapter 7.

Although popular romantic sentiment constructs the Aboriginal people as harmoniously fused with the land in a kind of religious ecstasy, the facts of Aboriginal society are far from this. Aboriginal people have been deprived of their land, their cosmology and their spiritual identity by the white invasion of this country. The degradation that can be witnessed in certain parts of Aboriginal society is living proof of the idea that when religious vision is lost, the people perish. It is thus grotesquely ironic to find white Australians projecting their own religiosity upon Aboriginals, when whites are themselves responsible for the loss of spiritual integrity in black culture. The degradation in Aboriginal society is actually a graphic mirror-image of what has already taken place in white society: loss of mythic vision and spiritual integrity, accompanied by a sudden and dramatic increase in violence, alcohol and drug abuse, social disorder, and individual disorientation.

White and black Australians today meet in the domain which Robert Johnson has called 'low-grade Dionysus'.[13] The loss of spiritual ecstasy in both white and black cultures has been replaced by the spurious, artificial ecstasy that is provided by alcohol and drugs. We can all get drunk together, and then have a bloody good fight at the end of it: this is one of the few forms of shared social ritual we still have left today. This is the side of outback Australia that I certainly did not miss when I left Alice Springs in 1972. I had seen too many brawls and punch-ups, too many white and black bodies careering through plate glass windows. Violence and destruction is the ultimate price paid by secularism: that part in us that demands ecstatic experience will take over, but in a wholly negative and brutal way. Instead of the controlled rituals of Dionysus, the mythic loosener of rational boundaries, we have the destructive boozing and brawling of Bacchus, a kind of debased or low-level form of Dionysus. White Australians *deny* the sacred, and many black Australians *have been denied* the sacred, but the result is the same: we both become the unconscious victims of inferior or unconscious ecstasy (interestingly enough, now the name of a very popular and harmful drug in this country).

'Ecstasy' comes from the root *ex statis*, to stand outside oneself. If we do not cultivate an other or outside place, a sacred place outside the ego, then inferior ecstasy will invade the body and the ego, destroying both in a horrifying fury, which one can witness most Friday nights outside certain pubs. We either sacrifice our pathetic rationality and get our spiritual and moral lives in order, or else irrationality will sweep over us in a reign of terror.

Perversely, when white Australians aspire directly to the sacred, to a larger reality which liberates us from the ego, this is ridiculed by our peers as 'escapist', unrealistic, or un-Australian (that imposingly fascist diagnosis). But the *negative* experience of otherness, the decentring of the ego provided through drugs and alcohol, is completely condoned and is seen as one of the institutional mainstays of the Australian way of life. From our own ignorance of the sacred and of its key liberating role in human life, we have made ourselves slaves to cheap and nasty episodes of ego-transcendence.

Resacralising as a social and political necessity

A living sense of the sacred is in this sense a hot sociopolitical issue: things simply go better in black or white society when a shared cosmology or mythic world-view is firmly in place. So many of our social and political problems stem from the loss or absence of a living and sustaining religious vision. This seems almost obvious and self-evident once it is stated: yet we do not find this sentiment expressed in most academic or intellectual research into Australian society and its social problems. This is because the anti-spiritual rationalistic temper already mentioned continues to dominate social and intellectual enquiry in this country. The ethics of individualism, libertarianism, and positivism will not allow researchers to argue in favour of mythic awareness or to point to the necessity of religious experience.

Apart from the alcohol and drug epidemic, the other urgent and pressing issues of the day share the same mythopoetic or spiritual background. Whether we turn to the need for a new ecological awareness or to the demand for reconciliation between white and black Australians, we can state categorically that neither of these enormous social problems can be solved by good intentions and force of will alone. A better ecological consciousness and better race relations require deep structural changes in the national psyche; both require that Australians develop a full and vital mythic awareness. In order to improve our environmental sensibility, Australians must develop a deeper, spiritual pact with the land, and be made to feel organically part of the land, so that nature is not continually damaged by an imperialistic ego that believes in the illusion of its own separateness. In relation to black–white 'reconciliation', I would argue that no true reconciliation is possible until white Australians have first reconciled themselves to the indigenous, mythically oriented person in their own souls. A great deal of inner work has to be done before the cultures can be meaningfully related. The new Mabo native land title legislation is a positive political sign that at least some whites are willing to accept the claims of their significant others, but unless this governmental initiative is complemented by conscious realisation and psychological experience it is in danger of remaining caught at a very superficial level. These subtle and complex issues form the bases for Chapters 7 and 8.

I want to argue that Australian society is now waiting on a change of consciousness which has still to occur. Some psychological movement is needed before our cultural life and our political 'reconciliations' can be furthered. It is the missing factor—the stone rejected by the builders of Australian society: namely, the mythic life and unattended religious feeling of Australians—which must now become the cornerstone of a revived and transformed political Australia. Here is a great and vivid example of how interdependent and organically related inner and outer worlds really are. Here is where mature and responsible development in the political Australia is intimately connected with the spiritual and psychological development of individual Australians. We are in a curious and vital place, where a mythopoetic revival is needed before our sociopolitical life can move forward.

The archaic dreaming soul, which is buried beneath the busyness of contemporary white rationality, is the missing ingredient necessary for Australia's psychological health and cultural stability. That dreaming soul is what we must integrate, not by way of consuming Aboriginality itself, but by way of cracking open our own consciousness to find the deeper, primal layers buried there, waiting to be released into life. Landscape is sufficiently powerful to be able to deliver the necessary blow to our consciousness, and thus create the opening through which the soul 'down under' can be born. My own experience of this quickening is recounted in the memoir that constitutes the following chapter.

1

A teenage alchemist in Alice Springs
A memoir

My soul is a strange country.
— RANDOLPH STOW[1]

I grew up in Alice Springs, central Australia, in the midst of Aboriginal culture. Thinking about Aboriginality is for me something more than a fashionable intellectual exercise; it is part of my childhood and adolescent experience, as well as part of my emotional being. During my years in Alice Springs I did not manage to find many conscious or deliberate inroads into Aboriginal culture, and I often had the feeling that the doors were closed to me. However, as will be explained, the impact of this ancient culture was more upon my soul than upon my intellect, more an emotional and psychic experience than it was a process of cultural exchange or of 'learning about' a different people. As a result, I had no real chance (apparently unlike the urban middle classes today) to actually appropriate their spirituality or to use their cosmology as a model or foundation for my own spiritual development. The impact of Aboriginality upon me was indirect, sideways, vague, and virtually wordless. It had nothing of the conscious chatter of a primitivist search after pristine cultures and primeval dreamings.

I had a few significant contacts with Aboriginal people, at school, on mission stations, and in adult work experience, but it was not the people so much as the Aboriginal *land* that had the real impact upon me. I am not wishing to disparage or downplay the people, only to be honest to my own experience in central Australia. The Aboriginal people can be seen as, and see themselves as, part of the symbolic continuum of the landscape, and so perhaps the usual Western distinction between people and land does not properly belong here.[2] By becoming attuned to the land, one is, almost involuntarily, becoming attuned to Aboriginality, or as it were to the 'source' of Aboriginality. I was aware, especially in my early teens, that Aboriginal people had something that I lacked: an intensely mythopoetic and sacred bond with the land. For me Aboriginality functioned rather potently as an example, or an image, of a spiritual pact with the land that I wanted to achieve. I did not, I could not, take on their particular cosmology as my own, but it served as a living reminder of the *possibility* of cosmology, and I know that my soul was stirred and inspired by the Aboriginal example.

I found out most about the Aboriginal animistic world-picture from a local white woman who seemed intensely alive and interesting to me, but who had been deemed eccentric by the town. She managed a sculpture-farm just south of Alice Springs, which featured the works of the sculptor of Aboriginal forms and figures, William Ricketts. Ricketts had told me, at his Melbourne 'Lyre-Bird Sanctuary' (in the Dandenongs), that he was 'Aboriginal inside'; he had a white man's body and an Aboriginal soul. Elsa Corbett lived alone on Pitchi Richi, a thirty-acre property teeming with Aboriginal faces made by Ricketts, and she taught me a great deal about Aboriginal myth, legend, and tribal custom. After being fired from my job as trainee accountant at the Alice Springs abattoirs (would I too, like Ricketts, go native?) she employed me, along with two Aboriginal men, to help maintain the extensive orange orchard. She took me around the MacDonnell Ranges and Mt Gillen district in a collapsing, near-derelict four-wheel drive, stopping to point out the significant geological features and telling me the Aboriginal stories that surrounded them.

She would indicate to which Dreaming, ant, emu, lizard, a certain pile of stones, waterless creek, or rocky ridge belonged. And who was I to question her authority? Some of it may have been invented on the spot, although she claimed to have been informed by traditional sources. But I suppose what mattered to me was that I was being exposed to a completely different mode of perception. The world was not just a static world of rocks, sticks, and earth, but a fluid world of imagination, capable of assuming a variety of shapes and many meanings. This budding mysticism, pantheism, or desert-romanticism deeply moved me, and had a lasting impact. It may not have been the anthropologically precise Dreaming to which Elsa Corbett exposed me, but it was, at the very least, the psychologically satisfying white man's dreaming, and landscape was never the same for me again.

Siege mentality in the outback

In Alice Springs the Aboriginal spirit of place is strongly felt. Again, I do not think this is a very conscious experience for whites; it is more a gut feeling or an instinctual response. More often than not, for many Euro-Australians, it sticks in the guts and makes them feel unpleasant, because it is threatening. Many of the whites I grew up with were passionate racists. Retrospectively, I can see that their racism was a futile defence against the sheer power of the spirit of place. In the deep outback there is an almost South African sense of siege; even though the actual numbers of Aboriginals are not always great, the very landscape, the backyard, the dirt sidewalk itself, tells white people that they are intruders and that their European culture and expectations are out of place. Urban Australians, especially those now rushing to consume Aboriginal cosmology, do not understand the psychic pressures exerted upon white people in the outback. The dreadful 'redneck' racism in the outback, which I grew tired of and was pleased to leave behind when I later moved south to Adelaide, is not the result of a conscious decision to hate a different people, but is an automatic and largely unconscious cultural defence against the power of the Other. Racism is no more excusable for this reason, but it is comprehensible in this context, and any attempt by governments or moral institutions to eradicate it must deal with the psychocultural forces that accompany and partly create it.

The spirit of place that challenges the Euro-Australian is an almost physical sensation in central Australia. I was fortunate in the sense that, unlike my own parents, I felt this sensation as a largely liberating, not threatening, force. Nor do I feel that my experience is unique; I noticed that a great many young people in Alice had a similar response to Aboriginality as myself, heralding a new era in race relations as well as in personal and cultural identity. Obviously I had less to lose than my parents. Being so young, I was not wholly identified with the European world-picture and its consciousness in the first place, so that when indigenous, non-European forces began to intrude upon or even replace parts of that consciousness this was as much cause for celebration as for reactionary concern and defensiveness. The young have a capacity to experience so-called alien forces and influences in a positive way, although when the young grow old they tend to experience the spirit of place in much the same way as their parents. In Alice Springs it will be the young who will refuse to grow old in the usual way, especially the artists, the drop-outs, and the *pueri aeterni* (Latin: eternal youths), who will gradually have an impact upon mainstream consciousness and alter its very structure and its defensive-aggressive underpinnings.

From the edge to the centre

I was born in the northern suburbs of Melbourne, at the edge of the island-continent, and so for me the symbolism of moving from the edge to the centre has always been important. When it was first suggested that our family would move from Melbourne to Alice Springs there was a good deal of fear and dread in all of us. The coastal fringe represented safety, the known, the civilised parts, and the interior was viewed as barren, scary, unknown. It was either not spoken about at all (an area of cultural silence) or it was viewed with a good deal of distaste as a place of death and disintegration. The centre was variously called the Dead Centre, the Empty Centre, the Desert Heart. As James McAuley put it, the outback was regarded as 'A futile heart within a fair periphery'.[3] A.D. Hope mythologised Australia as

> A woman beyond her change of life, a breast
> Still tender but within the womb is dry.[4]

Moving from the edge to the centre was therefore a movement from life to near-death, from richness to poverty, and, especially to me at the time, from a wonderful extended family network and human support to isolation, and to what Patrick White called the Great Australian Emptiness. The idea scared hell out of me, and I knew nothing of the sacred symbolism of the centre, nothing about the traditional notion of renewal and regeneration in the desert. Nor was I aware that for a long time before and even during the age of white exploration Europeans had projected the idea of paradise upon inland Australia.[5]

We moved to Alice Springs in the 1960s because of the

centre's renowned healing qualities. My sister had suffered from asthma in Melbourne since early childhood, and by the time she was sixteen the asthma was so bad and she was so debilitated that medical opinion warned she had only a few months to live. Our parents asked the surgeons at St Vincent's Hospital in Fitzroy what could possibly be done to help her. One suggestion, which they admitted at the time was a long shot, was to take my sister immediately to a drier climate, in the hope that this would heal the disorder, or at least extend her life-span beyond the projected few months. Mildura in north-western Victoria was the first place mentioned; then they seemed to agree that Alice Springs was the place to take her. Within a few weeks preparations were under way, and my mother and sister were to fly on a TAA 727 Whispering T-Jet to central Australia.

I went up with my father and my other sister later, by car, travelling along unmade desert tracks west of Lake Eyre in our egg-shell blue 1962 EJ Holden. It was not just a long trip or an epic journey, but an emigration. It seemed like a movement into another country, with vastly different landscape and different social ways, where we would live alongside a different race: the indigenous Australians, whom I had never seen before, except in picture postcards and on ashtrays and plastic boomerangs. They seemed to make up a goodly proportion of the town of then five and a half thousand people. The silence and remoteness of the land, the enormity of the stony gibber plains, the strangeness of the red earth and the brilliant sky, the occasional glimpse of wild horses and camels, of huge tumbleweed, of local dust storms, all of this both scared and attracted me. I felt like an alien, yet a deeper, more ancient part of me resonated to the ancient spirit of the place, and said: Welcome home, stranger.

My sister recovered from her serious condition within

six weeks and, miraculously, began to lead a new and fuller life in this remotest of places. While the family network here and back in Melbourne celebrated her recovery, the impact on me was slower, more subtle, yet no less profound. I began to be healed, not of pulmonary emphysema, but of the modern Western neurosis of alienation, brought about by the ego's tightness and rigidity, its refusal to acknowledge mythopoetic or archetypal forces beyond itself. The so-called death of God and the loss of religious sensibility has taken its toll on all of us: we have shrunk to the size of the mere human ego. I belonged to a Protestant family that still believed in God, but 'he' was far away, remote from us, and down here we lived as a bunch of small, tight, nuggety and squeaky-clean egos. We were, as Nietzsche might have said, human, all too human. We had no sense of self beyond the immediate conscious realm; we lived in human society but not in a spiritual cosmos, and we certainly felt no kinship or emotional identity with the land: our God was a distant sky-God, who did not appear to bless or enliven the created earth.

Landscape began to work on me soon after arriving in central Australia, and this took place about five years before my meeting with Mrs Corbett. While the asthmatic tightness in my sister's chest and respiratory system began to be relieved, I felt the habitual tightness of my closed ego begin to dissolve under the pressure, or the calling, of the seemingly limitless desert landscape. I felt enjoined to partly disidentify with the ego and to identify myself with, or to dissolve my identity into, the red, blue, and purple expanses around me. I had no language or framework for understanding what was happening at the time. Only occasionally an odd remark from a town drunk or an eccentric local would alert me to the fact that others, too, had a sense of expansiveness or a feeling of living beyond the normal limits of social identity.

We lived in the township of Alice Springs, but on the western edge of the town in a new area, within full view of Mt Gillen. Two or three blocks away from us the spinifex and semi-arid desert country started. You could probably walk from there to the Indian Ocean without being bothered by too many people. The land seemed to me to constantly point to, or hint at, other realities. The crumbling rocky ridges and tall ranges, the piles of rounded boulders and hills of granite, the fragmented sandstone and embankments of clay and ochre: all this seemed near-magical to me, to point to ancient civilisations or to worlds of other beings. I remember knocking on a pole with my shoe, hoping to discover the secret coded rhythm that would bring the invisible beings to light. I was delighted to find some time later that novelist Martin Boyd had felt the same way about Australian landscape:

> There is no country where it is easier to imagine some
> lost pattern of life, a mythology of vanished gods,
> than this most ancient of lands.[6]

The early British arrivals had called this country *terra nullius*, the empty land, but I found it teeming with mythic images, with sacred resonances, and with openings into other worlds. I suppose I scampered over rocks and explored gullies with the same enthusiasm that people nowadays reserve for their pilgrimages to the ruined temples and ancient cultural sites of Greece or Rome. Certainly I no longer felt I was in the middle of nowhere. The futile heart within a fair periphery had turned into a miraculous centre within a fairly ordinary edge. I felt I was somewhere special, in a cosmos of rock that was drawing me out of my habitual ego.

I sometimes felt that the rocky chasms and gorges would burst forth in song and praise. I remember one day, while exploring the plains at the foot of the MacDonnell Ranges, I found myself reciting lines, phrases, and prophets' names from the Old Testament. It felt rather odd, to bring the Bible into this country, but then, I pondered, this could well be Israel or the Middle East, and certainly the otherworldliness of the Holy Lands matched the otherworldliness of this place. I recall talking to my Sunday-school teacher about my feelings of central Australia, and asking him how we could relate this place to the Bible. He said that Australia was a sacred land and that it would one day give rise to a rebirth of the Holy Spirit. That gave me plenty to think about, but the next year he was arrested by police one Sunday morning in Todd Street. He was found walking naked through the centre of town, with a small band of black and white followers, and with his arms outstretched and singing songs of praise. He was gaoled, fined, and disowned by the John Flynn Memorial Uniting Church of Northern Australia. I got wind then of the dangers involved in opening oneself to the spirit of place and to the sacredness of landscape. I wanted to visit him at the gaol, but my parents forbade it. He was clearly a madman, they said. Why? I asked, and they both looked at me as if one day I would walk naked in near-ecstasy or madness through the town; as if perhaps I had caught the bug, and had listened too closely to what he had preached during all those Sunday-school classes.

Landscape as spiritual laboratory

At the age of fifteen I left Sunday school and the Church, and joined the Alice Springs Gem and Mineral Club, which met every second Sunday afternoon. After a couple of years I had boxes of low-grade minerals and chipped gemstones under my bed and at the bottom of the wardrobe. On rocky quartz plains east and west of Alice, we would all be head-down, small pick-axes in hands, looking for crystal formations, for colourful clusters of rock, for zircons, amethysts and garnets. Sometimes I would find iron pyrites and think I had found gold. Especially west of Alice, when confronted with a glittering field of quartz and mica, I would sometimes imagine that I had discovered Lasseter's fabulous reef.[7] Years later, reading Jung, I found that gold was the symbol of the soul and of the alchemist's spiritual quest. Years later as well, because our family did not talk about our ancestry, I found I was descended on both my mother's and my father's side from goldseekers and diggers, from poor folk from Ireland, England, and the Isle of Man, who came out to the Victorian goldfields in the late nineteenth century in search of their fortune. They did not find any gold, but they stayed on, and moved south to Melbourne.

So I shared with them both the desire for gold and the failure to find any. But I suspect that we were all engaged in a less tangible search, a search for alchemical or spiritual gold, and that our gold-digging and searching was in part a literal enactment of the quest for philosophical gold. We were searching for the soul, and it is interesting that the link across four generations of Australians was that our soul-making was conducted in direct relationship with the land. Whether at Bendigo, Maldon, Ballarat, or Alice Springs, we were all head-down reverent worshippers of the rocky earth, not finding the precious metal, but nevertheless becoming deeply acquainted and at one with the rocks, stones, and mythic openings of this ancient continent. We were all students of the spirit of place, rock-philosophers, or what D.W. Harding might call geopsychologists.[8]

I reject the fashionable and trendy idea that the first white Australians were merely malicious and uncouth invaders of this land, driven by an empty gold-lust. It is part of our habitual national self-flagellation that we have allowed ourselves to believe and perpetuate this entirely negative image. The time has come, I feel, to strip away our guilt and our self-loathing and to examine the past, not only for its criminal atrocities and its political errors, but also for its mythic and archetypal resonances. There are so many amazing resonances in our Euro-Australian heritage, our journey across vast seas in order to arrive at a topsy-turvy world in search of gold or paradise, that we hardly need to create literary fictions or fabrications to express the Australian soul. As Mark Twain famously remarked,[9] rich and fabulous fantasies are already embedded in our actual history and geography, and all we have to do is to extract and refine them, to care for them with the same care extended to gemstones embedded in matrices of rock. We have to stop the self-loathing long enough to attend to the flecks of gold, the soul-sparks or *silex scintillans* in our lived experience.

A Sydney colleague once said that whereas the old European alchemists made gold in their dark, vaporous laboratories and secret fabricated chambers, we in Australia make gold, or discover symbolical gold, by direct encounter with the landscape.[10] Our spiritual way here cannot be, as was said by Hermes Trismegistus and other real or legendary Europeans, an *opus contra naturam*, a work against nature. There is too much nature in Australia, too much rock, too much *prima materia* or untransformed matter. If we heroically pitted ourselves against nature here in a bid to transform nature into spirit, we would go mad, break down, or be consumed by nature. The entire heroic fantasy about subduing nature, conquering Gaia or controlling Mother Earth is a European fantasy, which can never work in Australia. This country demands a different archetypal style, a style that works with nature rather than against it. The very notion that spirit is opposed to matter cannot take root here. Our spiritual mode will have to be ecological, a work *with* nature, an *opus cum natura*.

In this important aspect we must take our cue from the Aboriginal people and not from Western Europe. Herein lies what must be regional, local, or particular about an Australian spirituality. We cannot simply import Judeo-Christianity into this country and think that this will suffice. It won't work, because it is based solidly on masculinist and dualistic notions of spirit and matter that can make little sense here. The Australian Way will have to be ecological, like the Aboriginal people themselves. The new spirituality that arises from Australian experience will, I believe, be precisely the kind of spirituality that will set a timely example to the rest of the world. It will be nonheroic and will not go the way of the now exhausted heroism of Western Europe or North America. It will not be patriarchal, because the Earth Mother is far too strong here. Any glance at Australian literature or culture indicates that, despite the fact that Australian social and political institutions are patriarchal, the underlying emotional and psychological structures are governed by the mother. The great Australian writers from Henry Lawson through to Patrick White are all sons of the mother, in both the personal sense of being mother-dominated as children, and in the archetypal or mythic sense of being 'loved sons' of the chthonic earth as mature artists.[11]

My own experience in Alice Springs taught me to love and respect the Earth Mother[12] in ways that I could not have achieved while living in Melbourne. It was the Earth Mother and her stony landscape that broke the encasement of my rational ego and drew me into a larger sense of identity, that opened up a dialogue between myself and the archetypal other. Naturally the vast expanses and the sheer weight of all this rock terrified me at times, and one can easily feel crushed by it. But Australian landscape is like the unconscious itself: if you respect it and realise the ego can never hope to assimilate, conquer, or transform it, you are allowed to survive. That is and must be our way, a humble aboriginal way, a shamanic way. Les Murray has said that the sheer space and size of this country is 'one of the great, poorly explored spiritual resources of Australia', since 'in the huge spaces of the outback, ordinary souls expand into splendid [forms]'.[13] Randolph Stow has pointed out that 'when one is alone with [the country], one feels in one way very small, in another gigantic'. The actual ego-personality is dwarfed and made to feel quite small and puny, but the soul leaps out of its human encasement and ecstatically unites with the greater world. 'Alone in the bush, with maybe a single crow ... a phrase like "liberation of the spirit" may begin to sound meaningful.'[14]

As the 1960s drew to a close I realised that these rocks that were shamanising my life were also caught up in other lives and other stories, in Aboriginal Dreamings that I could not properly access or understand. This did not bother me very much at the time, although all my political friends tell me it should have. But I had not yet been taught by university education to be guilty about being white, male, and Anglo-Celtic. I have always felt that the rocks and mountain ranges of central Australia were large enough to accommodate many Dreamings: perhaps a different dreaming for everyone who comes into geopsychical contact with them. The fact that there could be many Dreamings did not, for me, cancel out the validity or importance of my own or any other dreaming. The landscape itself was plural, ever-changing, a festival of light and rock, always different, and so naturally this complex world would give rise to many stories, to many myths of place. In my heart I realised the priority and respected the major status of the Aboriginal stories that had already accounted for the places that I mooned around as a boy. But I always felt, arrogantly perhaps, that there was still room for my own psychic participation in the land. It had already happened anyway, and it was not something I could call a stop to on political, ideological, racial, or any other grounds.

An often drunken urban Aboriginal man who went by the name of Charlie used to tell me that a giant spear-head made of pure gold was lying at the bottom of the rock-pool at Emily Gap, only a couple of miles from where we used to work together tending Mrs Corbett's orchard. It had fallen out of the sky, he said, when one of the ancestor-beings was returning to the stars. He said this with such conviction, lifting his head upward to the sky, his throat tightly drawn, that I almost felt like urging all my friends at the Gem and Mineral Club to start excavating the site immediately. It amazed me then that gold should play an important role in the traditional Dreaming—or was it merely the drunken urban day-dreaming?—of this Aboriginal man. I told this story some time later to the Austro-Celtic poet Vincent Buckley, who was drunk at the time. He was intrigued and asked if I could arrange for him to go into the outback and meet some of these people. He said we should go with a mate of his called Arthur Koestler, who also wanted to explore the deep outback. I said yes, but we never did carry it out.

I spoke to him about my experience in the outback because I had been deeply hurt by an essay he had written called 'Imagination's Home', where he claimed that Australia could never become for him a 'source-country'; a source of imagination and mythical resonance for poets.[15] He listed several reasons why this should be so, and why only Ireland for him could continue to feed his soul, his imagination, and his poetry. He looked somewhat baffled and intrigued as I spoke about my soul-experience in central Australia, almost as if I belonged to another world, and certainly to another generation or breed of Australians. As we spoke in a smoky bar-and-grill in Adelaide, and as he became progressively drunker, my mind went back to that long childhood trek from Melbourne to Alice Springs, the endless horizons of rock and dust, the glimpses of wild brumbies and teams of camels, and I knew then that that was the psychological barrier that separated us. Here was a Melbourne poet, still at the edge of this great continent, and, consequently, still excluded from its emotional and mythopoetic resources. He kept singing the praises of Ireland because, in a sense, he had never arrived in Australia. And here was I charged with the task of introducing him to the interior spirit of the place. I knew even then that I could never do it; it was too conscious, too wilful, too much the urban person on safari in the outback, in search of primal stirrings. But what had hooked him was this golden spear-head of Charlie's. I caught the sudden intensity in his eye, the surge of interest, and then I knew that Australia could easily have become a source-country for this poet if he had lived another life, if he had crossed that long geopsychical barrier that separates the edge from the centre.

From the centre to the edge

> Le centre du monde est partout et chez nous
> The centre of the world is everywhere and with us
> — PAUL ELUARD[16]

I left central Australia just over twenty years ago now, and since then I have been living once again at the edge of the continent, in Adelaide, Sydney, and presently Melbourne. Now, at the edge, I continually dream of the centre. Quite literally so, I dream of central or outback Australia several times every month. I most often dream of a journey into the continental interior, and of arriving at a settlement that is characterised by its striking harmony with the natural environment. This could be any non-coastal town, settlement, or outpost, but usually something in the dream is directly or indirectly suggestive of Alice Springs. There are always Aboriginal people in the dream, and sometimes I have journeyed long distances to meet them. In one dream I journeyed to Alice Springs to visit an unknown Aboriginal woman, whose face I could not make out as she was sitting in the shade under an enormous flowering gum tree. I felt frustrated sitting beside her, as she did not say anything, but just sat there, with some mysterious aura about her. Why had I come here? I said to myself. The conscious self or personal ego is often frustrated in my series of dreams of Alice Springs. Obviously, what the psyche takes me to this imaginal place for has little or nothing to do with satisfying the demands of the rational ego.

Once I was welcomed at the entrance of a bush settlement by the poet Les Murray, whose work I have long associated with the Australian spirit of place. Although also singing the praises of his ancestral Celtic places, Murray is completely and profoundly at home in Australia, and his poetry gives us perhaps the best clues yet about what a genuinely Euro-Australian spirituality will look like. Murray has long ago crossed the geopsychical barrier that separates town and country, surface and depth, European and Aboriginal, and those politically correct people who think that that barrier ought not be crossed tend to dislike Murray because he transgresses those barriers and inhabits a free mental space that many Australians want to disallow. 'Ah, you have come at last,' he said to me at the shady entrance to this bush place. This was, apparently, my home, or it would become so. Or rather, it is the home of my poetic self, that part of me that could, in the dream, be personified by Les Murray. He stands at the entrance, welcoming me back from the conscious edge of my existence to the unconscious centre from which poesis and creativity spring.

It is important not to think too literally about the centre, or the edge for that matter. Whenever I become overwhelmed by a terrible nostalgia for Alice Springs I will have a dream which indicates that it is not necessarily the town itself that is my goal, my psychological centre. The dreams are far more intelligent than the ego, and when the ego becomes too literal about its psychic attachments, the dreams will cut across this and spring something new upon the ego, to shock it out of the literal toward the metaphorical.[17] The psyche strives to encourage not literal attachments or obsessive fixations, but fluid and changing metaphorical awareness. So, in one dream, I journey to Alice Springs and realise, upon arrival, that it is not this place that I want. Instead, I travel west of Alice toward the sandstone ridges and the rounded granite boulders. I leave the bitumen road and walk toward a landscape of rocks. I study the light and contour of the rocks, looking deeply into the crevices, searching for some code or secret. I go off looking for deepening, not for a literal place.

Whenever I dream of the centre it usually means that I am too much at the 'edge' or on the surface of my own experience. There is a need for a deepening of experience, for finding a central core or fibre to the fabric of daily life. I am too much caught up in the ego and enmeshed in its strivings. This is why the journey to the interior can often be unpleasant for the ego, or why the personal self can feel frustrated when it actually 'gets' there. The journey is not conducted for the sake of ego but for the sake of soul, which is most often choked and blocked out by the daytime ego. In the night, when the ego's desire is suspended, then the soul enters its own territory and it is free to express its own longing. These recurring dreams indicate that there is not enough sacred space in conscious life, and that at the first opportunity psyche tries to flee the edge in search of a wider cosmos.

The corollary of this—the ego's tendency to flee the centre and rush for the edge—is itself the subject of another dream. On the main south road that leads away from Alice Springs toward Adelaide, there is an impromptu gathering of local people. A young man is giving a talk and he seems to be quite agitated. He is asking everyone why they always leave Alice Springs when they get time off work. He says he is sick and tired of the way people run off to Adelaide and other places as soon as they get the chance. 'Why can't we stay here? What's wrong with this place? Okay, I know it can get pretty rough here from time to time, and people do not like the violence. But we should make a special effort to improve the place and to want to be here.' At the end the crowd applaud him, and I for one certainly feel the sting of his words. This dream shows what happens every morning when I wake up from the dream. At the earliest opportunity, I desert the centre and head for the edge. Ego's desires take over as the day comes into focus; often I have not even the time to record my dream, let alone allow sacred or cosmic space to enter my daily routine. The violence mentioned is intriguing. Alice Springs is a violent place, or at least I experienced it as such as a youth. But the violence here may well refer to the psychological 'violation' of the ego by the reality of the soul. It hurts the ego to remain in sacred space, it cuts across the ego's wishes and is—at least apparently—detrimental to the ego's short-term goals. Even as I teach in my lectures the value and importance of psyche, soul, depth, I know from my own dreams that I will walk out on that depth whenever I can, and that my ego needs continually to be counselled, as by the boy in this dream, to stay with interior space and not desert it.

Touring the centre

While living and working in Alice Springs I would often wonder about all the tourists who would come flooding in, from the edge of this continent and from the edge of other countries, especially America. It was typical for the locals to dislike or even despise the tourists, who were sometimes called 'terrorists' because they came in such large numbers and seemed to virtually invade or take over the town. They moved in herds or flocks from one picturesque outback scene or 'beauty spot' to another, shooting reels of snaps, slides, and videos to show others when they returned to the edge. Although their so-called safaris could easily be ridiculed for their fixed itineraries, and rigid, safety-conscious programs, I always felt that there was something valuable in their tourism. They had probably come for what attracted me to the centre, for its archetypal otherness. They had all grown tired of life on the edge and wanted to see what was inside. They probably sought what their bus drivers, tourist guides, and neat motel rooms could not provide: a glimpse of reality beyond the ego. And yet, although they sought to break down the ego's barricades and defences, those barricades were actually extended into the geographical depths of the continent. So that tourism, while seeming to cater to the impulse to transgress boundaries, to free the self in the direction of the psychological interior, actually supported the defences and barricades that made such a transgression impossible. Even as a teenager, I found the herds of tourists rather sad, especially the jolly ones, the ones eager for adventure and dressed in safari suits. The impulse to shatter the ego's frame had brought them here, but no such shattering would take place.

I think of the herds of tourists whenever I become too literally attached to the centre. I think of the glossy picture postcards, the snaps of numerous gorges, chasms, and rocky clefts, and remember that these massive openings in the MacDonnell Ranges have not acted as mythopoetic openings to the otherworld for these people. I could return to my alchemical landscape and find that, if I remain too identified with the ego and its structures, this landscape would no more act as a laboratory of transformation for me than it would for them. It might be just scenery and beauty spots, not a landscape of the gods. But these great stone monuments *could* act as mythic openings, if we would but allow ourselves to be opened up by them. Whether this ancient land is sacred presence, or simply great scenery, depends almost entirely on the condition of the ego-personality that meets it. The sacredness of the centre becomes evident only when we achieve the courage to leave the psychological edge.

The Australian psyche

2

Descent into the unconscious

> I knew that Australia was the country of the
> Upside-downers. A hole, bored straight through the
> earth from England, would burst out under their feet.
> — BRUCE CHATWIN[1]

Depth psychological factors are involved in the creation of new societies, but they are difficult to isolate and often the last factors to be subjected to scrutiny. Transplanted colonial societies always experience destabilisation in the psychological sphere. As a society transplants itself from the old to the new world, the delicate and carefully maintained balance between the two psychic systems, between consciousness and the unconscious, is disturbed. Ego-consciousness, which in the old parent culture had become sophisticated and had achieved a fairly high degree of autonomy, is reined in suddenly by the unconscious, which becomes stronger and more demanding in the new psychocultural situation.

In early Australian experience, consciousness is weighed down by the demands of colonial society, by the impact of the pioneer setting and of life lived in the raw. Not only refined manners and tastes go out the window, but many conscious values, principles, and directions are sacrificed in the struggle to survive, to build a new material culture, and to cope with the new conditions. In Jungian archetypal terms, there is less emphasis on the onward and upward spirit, and more emphasis on instinct, biological demands, and the dictates of survival.

This reorientation is entirely normal and is experienced not only by colonial or once-colonial societies such as Australia, New Zealand, Canada, and the United States, but also by individuals and families who emigrate to new countries and who attempt to adapt to different social, geographical, and psychological conditions. In *Psychoanalytic Perspectives on Migration and Exile*[2] Leon and Rebeca Grinberg explore the case histories of several migrants and migrant families, examining the psychodynamic changes and the emotional traumas that are characteristic of any experience of migration. They found that in almost every case unconscious processes were intensified, which led to a disruption of consciousness. Either a neurotic condition or a breakdown ensued, or else, after a temporary upheaval, there was a restructuring and a transformation of the personality.

In any event, the experience of migration is decisive, and what occurs in this process cannot be adequately explained by resorting to the usual statements about culture-shock and geographical displacement. The depth psychological perspective can throw new and more penetrating light on this cultural phenomenon, and I think the study of Australian society in particular can be illuminated by viewing it as a basically migrant society, which is still involved in the ongoing psychodynamic problems wrought by migration. As the Grinbergs have eloquently written, 'Migration is such a long process that perhaps it never really ends'.[3]

The fortunate fall: down-to-earth and democratic
There are several ways to evaluate the impact of the activation of the unconscious in early Australian experience. In positive terms, we could say that the

transplanted consciousness has become more natural, robust, down-to-earth, enterprising, and practical. There is much that is reassuring and authentic about the changed environment. On the other hand, critics of early and of present Australian society can argue that it has fallen in moral worth, has become dominated and corrupted by mere instinct, that it has become rough and crude, insensitive to spiritual values, materialistic, brazenly physical and so forth. The spirit archetype, or at least that form of the spirit that was known to the parent culture, 'dies' in the new setting, descends into matter, and is temporarily eclipsed by natural demands.

In all colonial societies there is a counter-response to this lowering of the threshold of consciousness. Frontier societies throughout the world are typically inflexible and puritanical bastions of high moral culture. There is always a strong conservative element that defends the values of the old country against those of the new. Very often, however, the colonial high culture is far more reactionary, oppressive, and dictatorial than the conservative element in the parent culture.[4] The new moralism is worse than the old, insofar as it is established in reaction to the powerful new activation of the primordial unconscious. The stronger the upsurge of instinct in colonial consciousness, the more severe is the resistance erected to defeat it. This new puritanism will appear quite bizarre, almost a mock-parody of conservatism and, as such, it loses credibility and authority in the eyes of many people. The will of the 'folk' triumphs over the colonial high culture.

In Australian cultural history this marks the end of the neo-classical colonial period and the start of the new national phase, which lasted roughly from the late nineteenth century to the 1940s and was concerned primarily with the definition of so-called genuine culture and authentic values. These values are celebrated and championed in such classic nationalist works as Joseph Furphy's *Such is Life* (1903), Henry Lawson's *While the Billy Boils* (1896) and *The Country I Come From* (1901).[5] The former British high culture is relegated to the scrap-heap or is turned into a laughing stock and a source of ironic humour and scorn. The national period in Australia (as in Mark Twain's frontier America) was marked by a relaxation of colonial defences, increased instinctuality and eros, and a sense of having come 'down to earth'. In Australia the national phase manifests as a celebration of the common people, as a cultural revolution championing working-class values and ordinariness.

Some historians, such as Russel Ward in his classic *The Australian Legend*,[6] have argued that the impassioned turn toward social democracy and egalitarianism in Australia was due largely to our convict heritage, to the hatred and fear that emancipist convicts felt toward hierarchical authority, and to their noble desire to see a 'fair go' for all. Social background is crucial, but so too is the depth psychological situation, which to date has not been taken into account.

In my reading of our fierce democratic spirit, the former ego-consciousness, as well as the imported British superego, collapses, exposing the lower levels of the psyche and allowing what Jung calls the 'shadow' to come into view.[7] It would seem logical, given the highly structured, class-conscious and hierarchical nature of eighteenth- and early nineteenth-century British consciousness, to assume that the shadow-personality, which generally acts in a compensatory way to consciousness, would be anti-authoritarian, democratic, and egalitarian. In this sense, the great achievement of Australian society is perhaps less spectacular or glorious than it is inevitable. As the old consciousness disintegrated, the egalitarian and democratic shadow—or what is sometimes paradoxically called the 'golden shadow',[8] containing positive traits excluded from consciousness—came to the fore, becoming the new dominant of Australian consciousness.

It was especially apt that the emancipated or freed convict should personify and carry the new set of values. The shadow is very much the 'prisoner' of the former consciousness, mistreated and abused by the superego, and pushed down into the dark dungeons of the unconscious (into British prisons, hulls of ships, and finally expelled to Australia). Many have argued against Russel Ward's convict-based view of Australian democracy, but even if it lacks historical or social credence, one can see how suggestible and attractive the idea is from an archetypal standpoint. The idea of the unfairly treated convict, the person abused by British society but with a heart of gold, is one of the foundation myths of Australian society. If this myth were treated as a psychological narrative, and not only as a sociological hypothesis based on 'fact', then we might gain a deeper understanding of the psychological structure of Australian society.

One thing is sure: it was not political or social forces alone that ushered in the new democratic era, making Australia at the turn of the century one of the most advanced political democracies in the world. It was also the case that the psyche set out on a new course, since the trauma and disruption of migration allowed the positive shadow to be released into consciousness. Although written in a different context, James Hillman's words can serve almost as a credo for Australian experience: 'Integration of the shadow is an emigration. Not him to us; we to him. His incursion is barbarism, our descent is culture.'[9] Even the geographical journey to Australia from Britain, the fact that it involved a *descent* to the deep south, to 'Down Under',[10] adds to the persuasive metaphor that in founding Australian society Britain unwittingly initiated an undoing of its own consciousness and a development of its imprisoned shadow. Australia is in a number of senses the scorned or reviled offspring of the parent culture, thus explaining the terrible inferiority that Australia has suffered throughout its history, but also explaining the cocksureness and boastful arrogance of nationalist Australians. It is not only the convict origins that stain our past, but also the ever-present awareness that we were actually born out of darkness in an archetypal sense. We were the children of darkness who were archetypally charged with the mission of bringing a new light into the world—hence the boastful assertions of superiority, when underneath we continue to be plagued by inferiority.

The not-so-fortunate fall: despair, violence, and oedipal rage

'So much horror in the clear Australian sunlight!'
— DOUGLAS STEWART, *Ned Kelly*[11]

The descent to the shadow is nevertheless a cultural decline as well as a *felix culpa* (a fortunate fall) to a new state of political grace. The Australian experience is not as clear-cut as Hillman's saying suggests: we experience *both* an increase in culture *and* a certain degree of barbarism. Many things were lost by the descent: high culture, the stable (if static and restrictive) superego, the civilised restraint on instinctual life, the certainties and structures of the past, the heroic thrust of the ego, and especially spirituality, the life of the spirit, and appreciation of the non-material.

The things lost, as well as the things gained, have been memorably articulated in the stories and other works of Henry Lawson, the most famous and accomplished figure of the nationalist period. Lawson's stories depict the grandeur of a new political order, a vision based on solidarity, mateship, human feeling, and egalitarianism, if at times Lawson questions the actuality of this new vision. But his works also reveal a sense of nostalgia for a lost past, which is associated with civilisation, high culture, and refinement. This nostalgia is not, as some have suggested, Lawson's personal hankering after a lost ideal, but rather the expression through him of the new nation's dawning awareness of the loss that its new consciousness has entailed. Furthermore, in Lawson there is a perception that Australian society is perched on the edge of an abyss. This abyss is projected upon the landscape, which is experienced as threatening, a malign force that would actively destroy its Euro-Australian inhabitants.

Here is the disintegrative aspect of the archetypal descent expressed as a strangely negative 'spirit of place' or as a disturbing quality of the Australian landscape. Lawson sees Australians in a state of real spiritual and existential danger, a people without meaning and direction other than the social and political meaning that the helpful shadow is able to provide. The shadow's political message of solidarity and social unity is not enough: it makes for a good society but not for culture in the fullest or deepest sense of the term. What I am describing here was put succinctly by Sir Keith Hancock in 1930: 'For nationality consists not merely in political unity but in spiritual achievement. Regarded from this point of view the Australian people have not yet come of age'.[12]

There is real desperation and despair in Lawson, making him, in my eyes, all the more deserving of his legendary status. Yet he has most often been celebrated for only one part of his achievement: for his recognition of the political and social progress of the Australian people. But his perception that we have at the same time fallen into a spiritual depression, that we lack purpose other than the cheery workaday purpose of social democracy, has not been noticed, or only obliquely and grudgingly. Lawson has been hailed as the 'apostle of mateship' but not as the prophet of our existential plight. He is too often read and enjoyed (especially in our school system) with blinkers on, with no regard for the existential doubt and gloom that can be found even in his lightest sketches. Where noted, his darker side is felt to be the product of his personal quirkiness, or even of an inherited, biological melancholia and depressiveness (as in Colin Roderick's biography of Lawson).[13] Australians will take full possession of the bright and positive aspect of Lawson as a reflection of their own national character—and so declare this aspect 'truly Australian'—but the dark and despairing side, the nostalgia for what has been lost, the spiritual malaise, is regarded merely as his personal problem and subjective weakness.

Lawson's contemporary, Barbara Baynton, paints a bleak and sometimes even demonic picture of Australian society. Hers is a human world that has fallen to a level below that of the animal. Dogs, sheep, and cattle show signs of faithfulness and moments of warm affection, but not so the human figures who are found in her *Bush Studies* (1902).[14] They are crude, raw, and impulse-driven creatures capable of appalling aggression and violence. Baynton's Australia shows the incursion of, or descent to, the shadow as apparent barbarism. Her portrait is extreme and ought to be regarded not as social realism but as symbolic or psychological realism, as fiction that expresses what lies below the social veneer of a colonial society. But her work is nonetheless 'Australian' and does represent a significant part of the Australian psyche. With Baynton too, critics and nationalists have tried to argue that her morbidity is entirely personal, a result of her psychic instability and mental illness, which she has merely projected upon the Australian scene. In some quarters there is almost indignation: how dare she inflict her private neurosis upon a healthy and growing society. It is wrong to pretend that her darkness is un-Australian, and certainly misleading to contrast—as is so often done in period studies of the 1890s—her 'darkness' with Lawson's 'light', especially when there is so much unacknowledged darkness in Lawson's own work.

While the positive or helpful shadow is personified and ultimately mythologised in the figure of the nation-building emancipist convict, the blacker and more violent side of the Australian shadow is personified in the bushranger, highwayman, or dangerous robber. This familiar figure in Australian writing and folklore is crude, coarse, all-male, and angry. He feels he has been deeply wronged by society and so he feels licensed to 'let the bastards have it', to transgress the law and to hack away at the apparently corrupt establishment. Here the interaction between the old superego and the uprising and rebellious shadow assumes the form of an oedipal conflict between the symbolic father or paternalistic authority and the struggling and unfairly treated son. Australian literature and history are littered with instances where the rebellious youth or *puer aeternus* attempts to fight the negative father or *senex*, who appears variously as hard-line police, merciless magistrates, self-serving squatters, or simply as 'the system'. As bushranger, the youthful shadow-figure is not nation-building or constructive, but immoral and destructive. He is the unsavoury and not-so-golden shadow, the shadow that British consciousness felt justified in repressing and punishing. But it is also *through* the archetypal perspective of the malign shadow or rebellious youth that British consciousness looked upon Australia and its currency lads as a whole, finding the South Land repugnant and not noticing (at least, not at first) the great psychological and social experiment that was taking place here.

Although the bushranger, and to a much lesser extent the local larrikin or prankster, was a menace to law and order, 'the folk' could not condemn him because he embodied significant qualities of the Australian psyche. He acted out on the social stage the release of oedipal rage, primal narcissism and the attempted defeat of an apparently repressive, paternalistic system. Thus the bushranger, who often acted gratuitously and for mere self-gain or exhibitionist display, was sometimes idealised inappropriately as a people's hero, as a Robin Hood driven by a higher morality to depose the system on behalf of the oppressed and mistreated majority. In the 1870s Ned Kelly emerged as a living legend because he embodied this archetypal pattern, which was so fundamental to Australian psychology. He was angry, young, rebellious, and he was said to have a just cause: he and his fatherless family had been mistreated by police, his mother had been imprisoned by patriarchal law and the whole system seemed corrupt. Kelly was authorised by the folk and the archetypal shadow to wage a guerilla war on the establishment.

It is significant that Kelly, his gang, his family, and many of his sympathisers were Irish or Irish-descended, and that the troopers were English, English-descended, or *constructed* as English even when they were not. Englishness in colonial Australia was equated with the repressive superego and the negative father to be overthrown, while Irishness then (and still today) represented the maligned and creative Oedipus or *puer* who would finally come into his own in a land far removed from British injustice. It is true that Australian society inherited the age-old political debacle between England and Ireland, which was concretised in the fact that so many of the early convicts were Irish while their gaolers were English, but this conflict between nations is firmly based on archetypal factors, and it is the psychological aspect of this ongoing *senex–puer* rivalry that concerns us in this context. There is a wealth of literary, filmic, artistic, and other works on the Kelly gang and bushranging, but only Douglas Stewart's play *Ned Kelly* (1943), Sidney

Nolan's series of Kelly paintings (1946–55), and Robert Drewe's novel *Our Sunshine* (1991) have begun to unravel the psychological and symbolic structure within this popular folk legend.[15]

We have seen how difficult it is to separate the negative from the positive shadow in Australian experience. In practice these two psychological aspects are always so closely related that Australian experience can only be comprehended in paradoxical terms. The Australian shadow is both liberator and destroyer: it liberates the repressed life, it brings on the democratic spirit, and yet it lowers the level of consciousness and releases the primitive, collective forces of the psyche. Its mission is always double-sided and Janus-faced. And yet official Australian culture and the national sentiment of the folk will mostly want to emphasise the good and to skew the shadow archetype toward the positive. Hence, in Australian folk culture, the shadow-figures are all basically 'good boys': the convict is viewed as unfairly punished for small misdemeanours, or more sinned against than sinning; the bushranger is rarely viewed as an antisocial brute but mostly as some kind of working-class hero. Lawson's writings are read solely in terms of their promotion of mateship and defence of democracy, and Barbara Baynton's contorted, gothic shadow-world is read merely as the reflection of a disturbed mind: in these and other ways the national shadow is hygienically removed.

Jung and Lawrence: the old-world critique of new-world democracy

> The instinct of the place was absolutely and flatly democratic, *a terre* democratic. Demos was here his own master, undisputed, and therefore quite calm about it … It was a granted condition of Australia, that Demos was his own master.[16]

C.G. Jung and D.H. Lawrence both provided depth psychological critiques of 'new-world democracy'. Jung felt that in American cultural experience there had been a certain primitivisation of the American mind, brought on by a new and sudden contact with the energies of the deep unconscious. In 'The Complications of American Psychology' (1930) Jung argues that colonial societies are invariably forced into new and potentially dangerous encounters with the primordial psyche, since the very act of uprooting and transplanting a culture tends to weaken and dislodge consciousness while the unconscious is stirred to new activity. Colonial or new-world societies tend toward democracy and egalitarianism, Jung felt, not because of any high-minded philosophy or spiritual principles, but because the *collective* layers of the psyche have been strengthened, giving rise to collectivist attitudes, values and considerations.

Lawrence felt the same way about the fierce democratic spirit in Australia. For him it was an essentially regressive phenomenon because Australian democracy seemed not so much to champion the people as to diminish and weaken the individual. Jung and Lawrence feared new-world democracies for their anti-individualist tempers, and both favoured old-world European individualism, seeing democracy as the result of a descent rather than an ascent of the human spirit. Lawrence felt that the 'aggressive familiarity' that the Australian democratic temper promotes is antithetical to the spiritual life of man, since the spirit demands a sense of otherness or aloofness from the merely mundane, and any culture that values spirit must grant or recognise something 'innate, sacred, and separate'[17] in human nature. It is not that Jung or Lawrence were opposed to democracy *per se* as a governmental structure, but that the equalitarianism that new-world societies generated tended to have a levelling or downward influence, so that the lowest common denominator held sway.

Jung wrote that in American society

The overwhelming influence of collective emotions spreads into everything. If it were possible, everything would be done collectively, because there seems to be an astonishingly feeble resistance to collective influences.[18]

This could readily be dismissed as right-wing reaction to, or distaste for, socialist elements, but I think it is unfair to treat these comments in this predictable way. Although many think of Americans as individualists, it is true that they are tremendously swayed by public opinion, the mass-media, fashion and trends, and are psychologically 'suggestible' to the collective. In colloquial language we might say: they are doing their own thing together. To an old-fashioned Swiss-German individualist, the American social experiment seemed alarming and repugnant. Every 'private' emotion and 'personal' ambition seemed to have its origin in public opinion and the media. 'You are simply reduced to a particle in a mass, with no other hope or expectation than the illusory goals of an eager and excited collectivity,' Jung argues, and he concludes:

You feel free—that's the queerest thing—yet the collective movement grips you faster than any old gnarled roots in European soil would have done.[19]

'You feel free in Australia', writes D.H. Lawrence in *Kangaroo* (1923), and here the great contemporaries converge in expression as well as thought (Jung's 1930 essay was written in English): 'You feel free in Australia. And so you do. There is a great relief in the atmosphere, a relief from tension, from pressure. But what then?'[20] Lawrence points out that boastful Australians love to tell foreigners and visitors that theirs is a 'free country', but he questions the meaning of this supposed 'freedom' in a country given over to what he calls 'herd-unity, equality, domestication'.[21] Like Jung, Lawrence records with a condescending humour the antics of new-world mass-mindedness: 'They all rushed from where they were to somewhere else, on holidays'.[22] Jung claimed that the individual is reduced to a 'particle in a mass' in America, and for Lawrence the individual in Australia is turned into a 'bit of the collective':

> The people of this terrestrial sphere are all bits. Isolate one of them, and he is still only a bit. Isolate your man in the street, and he is just a rudimentary fragment ... He's only a bit, and he's only got a minute share of the collective soul ... Never a thing by himself.[23]

Lawrence's novel *Kangaroo* is understandably hated by many Australians because of stinging attacks such as this on the Australian national character and way of life. But once you get over the insult, Lawrence has a real point. Australians valorise and celebrate democracy without thinking of its shadow aspect. We are taught to believe that democracy is an ultimate value or ideal, a veritable god, before which we will lie down and die. Those who dare to criticise democracy are viewed as horrible fascists, or at least as snobs and elitists.

But the levelling influence that has taken place in Australian society under the banner of 'democracy' cannot be denied. The downward tug of the shadow and the unconscious (Neumann calls this 'psychic inertia'[24]) has linked us to instinct, collectivity, and each other, but the cost to individuality and to the individual spirit has been considerable. To assert one's individuality and genius in Australia is, as Lawrence saw and knew, one of the cardinal sins of our society. The disadvantaged person here is the exceptional person, the talented individual. Anyone who stands out above the crowd is a threat to the clan and to the 'herd-unity' or frail stability of the young nation. Any tall poppy in this garden of enforced equality is liable to incur the wrath of the collective and to be lopped. We have characterised this behaviour as the 'Tall Poppy Syndrome', and although contemporary Australians are capable of making fun of their capacity to 'lop the big ones', they keep lopping just the same. It must be seen not just as an isolated, grotesque sport in its own right, but as part of the democratic complex of the country. The negative face of *demos* is surely conformity, mindless collectivity, standardised behaviour, and aggressive hatred of whatever rises above the norm.[25] Jung wrote that collectivisation is responsible for 'a flattening influence on people's psychology',[26] and this too finds an echo in Lawrence's phrase that Australia is 'flatly democratic'.

It should be pointed out, finally, that America and Australia have enjoyed completely opposite and antithetical kinds of mass-mindedness. The upbeat, heroic American temper has led to a different kind of collectivity from the down-beat, antiheroic Australian sensibility. Americans adore being successful, collectively, together. If it were possible, every American would be a star, a hero, or a millionaire. Australians prefer it if everyone is as undistinguished as everyone else. The maxim in this country appears to be: 'There are no stars in our team'. We see this most clearly in Australian sporting life: highly talented players cannot afford to draw too much attention to themselves, but must submerge their identity in that of the team. Heroism and individual achievement are frowned upon and are cause for embarrassment; team spirit or 'mateship' is the national ideal. The stifling side of this code of conduct is readily experienced by those who dare to challenge these assumptions. Alienation and ostracism are found all too frequently in this democratic and fair nation, since the finer print reads: You can only be my mate so long as you act the same as I do.

The Australian masculinist character as national defence

> For man has closed himself up, till he sees all things thro' narrow chinks of his cavern.
>
> — WILLIAM BLAKE[27] (on Ned Kelly?)

It could be argued that the Australian national character is based on a series of fundamental denials and on the one-sided promotion of the golden aspect of the shadow. There is little room in the nationalist ethos for Baynton's violence, Lawson's despair, Ned Kelly's narcissistic rage, or Lawrence's perception of the flattening and destructive influence of the Australian temper. The nationalist character wants to emphasise the anti-authoritarian egalitarian shadow, and lay claim to such classic traits as earthiness, unpretentiousness and pragmatism, but refuses to acknowledge the dangers and problems wrought by this lowered threshold of cultural consciousness.

If our consciousness is situated, metaphorically, below sea-level, and is therefore subject to flooding by the unconscious, then the nationalist character sets about erecting strong barricades and bulwarks, artificial defences to keep the unconscious at bay. Hence the 'typical' or preferred national ego comes to construct itself as strong, tough, and stoical. Enormous energy is exerted in the construction and maintenance of resilient barriers against emotion, against feeling, against any kind of inwardness, since what is 'inner' comes to be associated with what is dangerous, what undermines and makes us feel weak. So the classic Australian becomes stoical, resistant to feelings; and laconic, resistant to the expression of feelings and emotions in language, behaviour or culture.

Australian consciousness (and here I am referring both to men and women) has constructed itself as masculine in the symbolic or archetypal sense. But the masculinity is exaggerated and hollow, a kind of parody of masculinity, since the archetype that produces authentic masculinity—the archetype of spirit, which is mythologically associated with the father—is missing. Australian men develop a sort of false, forced, or extreme masculinity, and this serves merely to mask their sense of inner weakness and vulnerability.[28] They are archetypally sons of the mother, due to their natural proximity to the maternal unconscious and to their continual attempt to kill off the father, and yet they strive to present themselves as masculinist creatures. The 'typical' Australian male, whether we talk about the bushman, the battler, the larrikin, or the suburban ocker, understands masculinity as machismo and thinks that 'being masculine' means being tough, forceful, and aggressively defensive.[29] It is a forced, adolescent style of masculinity, one which desires to prove itself in rituals of combat and battle, both locally in pubs and on sports fields, and overseas in exotic theatres of war.

Australia rapidly became a so-called 'real man's' country, and women too were forced to adopt defensive strategies and a 'tough' consciousness. Here is where the Jungian reading of Australian cultural experience departs slightly from classical feminist readings of the construction of gender identity in this country. The feminist viewpoint contends that women have been programmed by a male-dominated society, which determines and controls the political messages of the culture, to abdicate their feminine values and sensibilities in order to better serve the patriarchy. The depth psychological viewpoint, however, shifts the perspective to another level: women have been conditioned more by the internal and psychological forces of a national psyche obsessed with masculinity than by external forces of sociopolitical propaganda. There are, of course, ways in which feminist and depth psychological readings can be brought together, so that political and archetypal factors can both be seen to play determining roles in the construction of women's experience.

One fascinating feature of Australian cultural history is the phenomenon of women 'dressing up' as men, living as men, and wishing to be seen as male by the society. Examples of such cross-dressing can be found in Furphy's *Such is Life* and in Eve Langley's *The Pea-Pickers* (1942).[30] The political reading of this is that woman, in a male-dominated context, is underprivileged and discriminated against; if she poses as a male these oppressions might be avoided and a new freedom attained. However, another reading might be that she is responding unconsciously and quite literally to the intensified masculinity of the cultural ethos, that by cross-dressing and by crossing the gender border, she is entering more fully into the psychosocial condition of her time. I use this example simply as an indication of the masculinisation of Australian society, a process that appeared to coincide with, and to be institutionalised by, the development of the nationalist character.

It appears that 'femininity' in society, in men and at least in some women, was given a markedly negative evaluation—a situation that only now is changing as Australia moves into a new cultural phase. As the Australian psyche matures, macho-masculinity will be outgrown, and the culture will turn to, re-evaluate, and look for new direction from, femininity. This turn toward the feminine is already well under way, at least among educated Australians, and the macho-style is being parodied and made the subject of social humour. As the conventional consciousness becomes self-conscious, it will be sensed more and more as inauthentic, false, as restraining rather than as expressing life.

I would argue that at the high point of Australian nationalism, neither femininity nor masculinity was known or fully experienced because what was in the ascendant was a hypertrophied or exaggerated masculinity. The experience of masculinity and of femininity as archetypal principles was eclipsed by the psychological need to create barriers of defence and a sort of siege mentality. A pioneer society defends not only against the assault of the elements, against famine, flood, heat, drought, fire, and Aboriginals, but also against the new unconscious forces that it has involuntarily unleashed. The national defensive habit has much in common with what Alfred Adler called 'the masculine protest',[31] namely an exaggerated attitude of strength and power adopted by a weak or vulnerable part of the psyche in order to ensure its continuation and survival. Adler noted that, although the masculine protest sometimes served short-term needs well, it could not be sustained long before exhaustion and collapse set in.

As well as denying or defending against disruptive emotions there is also the spontaneous cultural activity of projecting negative psychic contents upon other things and other people. In Australian experience, Aboriginals, women, individualists, foreigners, and landscape are all carriers of negative psychic images. They often carry the harmful or threatening contents, which are not recognised as aspects of the Australian psyche, as disturbances within itself. Hence endemic to the nationalist ethos, which is espousedly so generous and accommodating, so fair-minded and democratic, are racism and racial violence, xenophobia, homophobia, misogyny and other forms of projective paranoia. There is always something 'out there' that seems to threaten the nationalist ego's freedom, whether the Chinese ('the invading yellow peril'), women ('always conniving to trap a man and bring him down'), Aboriginals ('untrustworthy and animalistic savages'),

Americans ('they'll take us over if we let them'), or the landscape, often depicted in our early literature, and especially in Lawson, as an actively malign force bent on ruining the ego's ideals, dreams, and aspirations. The apparent confidence and self-satisfaction that the nationalist ego and its 'bush culture' espouse is a sort of fool's paradise, which is undermined from within by all that is repressed and denied in its own situation.

As Freud and his followers discovered, the rigidly defensive ego-personality thrives on projective paranoia and dissociative strategies in order to force outside the self those disruptive elements that attack it from the inside. Thus in nationalist Australia, negative projections, scapegoating, acts of emotional or physical violence, attempts to subdue the other, are frequently indulged, while all the while the nationalist ego considers it is living in 'the worker's paradise', in the best of possible worlds.

The psychological uses of landscape

A defensive cultural consciousness can do remarkable things with landscape. The landscape can act (as in Henry Lawson) as a field for negative psychic projections, where the land becomes constructed as an 'Out Back Hell' against which the enfeebled ego must defend itself. But we can also find a completely different psychological 'use' of landscape in Australian nationalist culture, with roots going back to Henry Kingsley's colonial romance *Geoffry Hamlyn* (1859)[32] and beyond. This involved the representation of Australian landscape as a rural paradise or Arcadia. In this second tradition, the ego does not project the unconscious outward upon the land, but rather converts the land into an image of itself, or into an idyllic field that serves the ego's growth, meets its needs, and reflects an image of stability, peace, and security. The motto of this Arcadian tradition might well be Freud's famous dictum: 'Where id was, there ego shall be'.[33]

The nationalist folk-image of the 'Bush' is a comforting and familiar construct in which Euro-Australians feel at home and with which they emotionally identify. This is the world of Adam Lindsay Gordon and of the so-called 'Bush School' of writers. The emphasis in Gordon's poetry, for instance in 'The Sick Stockrider', is on naming the landscape, on converting the unknown into familiar properties, selections, and cattle-runs, each with friendly-sounding and often familiarly English titles. The message was clear: this land is our land, we live in it, and have taken possession of it in the name of Euro-Australian society.

The great master of this art of cultural appropriation and psychological imperialism was A.B. (Banjo) Paterson,[34] whose works are central to the production of the nationalist character. His legendary 'The Man from Snowy River', 'Clancy of the Overflow', and 'The Man from Iron Bark' constructed the landscape as a glorious and sweeping backdrop to the activities and achievements of rugged, resourceful Australian men. His portrait of the Bush as an ego-syntonic field so completely met the needs of a vulnerable, nascent consciousness that the folk quickly adopted Paterson as their hero and enshrined him as the 'Banjo of the Bush'. On the other side of the spectrum was Henry Lawson, similarly revered, not for his dystopian landscapes but for his cheery expression of national ideals, new social values, and humorous sketches of Bush life.

The conflict between utopian and dystopian images of Australian landscape came to an interesting climax in the *Bulletin* literary debate or verse-argument between Paterson and Lawson in 1892–93. Lawson started the debate with 'Up the Country', a refutation of Paterson's Arcadian Australia and targeted at the idyllic world of 'Clancy of the Overflow'. Paterson countered with 'In Defence of the Bush', and Lawson rejoined with 'The City Bushman', where he argued that the romantic image of the Bush was a product of the city, invented by those who do not venture into the Outback, and who are unaware of its 'real' nature. 'We wish to Heaven', Lawson wrote in 'Some Popular Australian Mistakes' (1893), 'that Australian writers would leave off trying to make a paradise out of the Out Back Hell; if only out of consideration for … the lost souls [who live] there.'[35]

We have to do here with two psychological scenarios, both arising from the same defensive consciousness but leading to opposite cultural outlooks and different relations to the environment. Is the unconscious to be made visible, to be represented as a 'foreign' landscape, and to be battled against by a siege mentality? This is the embattled style of Lawson, and a profitable mode for art and artists since so many inner conflicts can be given expression by emotive representations of landscape. Or is the unconscious to be denied, and the land declared free of alien spirits; the country converted into a land of industry and human commerce? This is the confident, optimistic style of Banjo Paterson, creator of the 'jolly swagman', and a profitable mode for nationalists and politicians, since social development is more readily encouraged where the spirit of place is perceived as inviting and congenial. In Joseph Furphy's *Such is Life* (1903), the nationalistic Tom Collins boasts that Australia is a free and 'recordless land', a country of the future with great potential for growth since it is devoid of spirits, presences, and the past, or as Collins puts it, 'is clogged by no fealty to shadowy idols'.[36]

Nationalism waved a wand over the landscape of the Aboriginal dreaming and turned it into real estate and natural resource. A good example of this magical activity is W.C. Wentworth's long poem 'Australasia' (1823), in which he celebrates how 'the mournful genius of the plain' is 'Driv'n from his primal solitary reign', and in place of the *genius loci* he saw 'The cheerful villas 'midst their wellcropp'd land'.[37] A few years earlier, in prose, Wentworth had performed the same cultural exorcism in favour of the hegemonic ego: 'What a cheering prospect for the philanthropist to behold what is now one vast and mournful wilderness, becoming the smiling seat of industry and the social arts; ... to hear the joyful notes of the shepherd ... instead of the appalling yell of the savage, and the plaintive howl of the wolf'.[38] Always the nationalist temperament constructs the *otherness* of the landscape as appalling, mournful, and replaces it with a 'cheerful', 'smiling' world based on the ego's values. The fact that the new social order is entirely oppositional to the spirit of place is revealing of the defensive nature of the nationalist programme. It goes without saying that the 'civilising' project, and its aggressive attack on the 'genius of the plain', gave the colonising ego the same authority to banish the indigenous people and to 'drive' them also from the land. Where Aboriginality was, there Europe-in-Australia shall be.

A.G. Stephens of the *Bulletin* developed an ingenious strategy on the eve of Australian federation. He decided that the strangeness of the Australian landscape never existed, and that the perception of these qualities was part of 'the grotesque English prejudice against things Australian'. He was so infused with the utopian temper, and with the ego's colonisation of place, that he believed that seeing the land 'through clear Australian eyes' would reveal a country of immense beauty and cheerful demeanour. Stephens averred that there was one 'honest Englishman', and that was Henry Kingsley, who demonstrated his 'honesty' by portraying Australia as a magnificent Arcady, a place covered in flowers, filled with 'aromatic perfume' and containing many delights and surprises.[39] The archetypal image parading as 'reality' here, and putting itself forward as the 'commonsensical' view, was undoubtedly that of the earthly paradise, the desired setting, or *background*, for the birth of the most advanced social democracy. The so-called 'Bush tradition' was not especially interested in the 'bush' at all, not as a natural world in its own right, but merely as a sort of heraldic or emblematic context for major political transformations.

Paterson's Arcadian landscape was perhaps the 'real bush' for many Australians a hundred years ago, when the vulnerable ego needed to be bolstered and made secure. But Lawson's Australia resonates more for us today, not because it provides a negative view of place, but because it treats the land as other, as mysterious and irreducible other. A century after the defensive and limiting frame of high nationalism, we are today in a more expansive mode, and are looking to the landscape, and to Aboriginals, as sources of mystery and otherness. We look for hints and clues about the Australian unconscious, about 'other' histories and realities, not for self-confirmation or consolidation of the ego.

Imminent cultural change

The end of the twentieth century is a time of enormous change and upheaval within Australian society. The masculine protest, so contrived, and, as Adler astutely noted, ultimately so fragile and temporary, has begun to break down, and with it the aggressively defensive persona that it gave rise to. This crumbling of our psychological stockade has been in evidence for some time, at least since the end of the Second World War and certainly since the time of the Vietnam War. Contemporary Australian literature has been tearing away at conventional attitudes and subverting local mores and values since the 1960s and '70s. It would be wrong to see this writing as merely a protest literature, because the destructuring that is now taking place is occurring at the very centre of our culture and cannot be confined to the margins. Many Australians are today bored with their own self-imposed confinement and defensiveness, and are eager to explore what lies beyond our traditional barricades and defences. Many are alert to the false unity imposed upon the country by nationalist sentiment, and are keen to explore ruptures and gaps—both within society and the self. There is a new receptivity to plurality and otherness, especially as these are embodied in women, Aboriginality, multiculturalism and Asia-Pacific neighbours. (These changes will be further discussed in Chapter 6.) Meanwhile, a good many other Australians, especially in our folk- or low-culture, want to continue as before, nationalistic, contracted, suspicious of foreigners, masculinist, devoted to closure, unity, certainty.

This situation is ironic because in the nineteenth century it was the colonial high-culture which was felt to be moribund and obsolete, whereas the egalitarian low-culture was progressive and forward-looking. The new postcolonial and post-stockade ethos in Australia is being brought in as it were from above. With these changes taking place at a furious rate, with people from the city and country being exposed to a post-masculinist consciousness that encourages openness and is suspicious of closure, the old nationalism is under threat. But then, threat is what it is used to and what it has come to expect, because the siege mentality is its forte.

3

The need for sacrifice

Out on the wastes of the Never Never —
That's where the dead men lie! ...
That's where the Earth's loved sons are keeping
Endless tryst ...

— BARCROFT BOAKE[1]

Contemporary white Australians feel profoundly unsettled and unsure of themselves. Today we find very little of the bumptious and self-promoting nationalism that has been strong in the past and that once provided a foundation for national and personal identity. In sports arenas we still shout 'Come on Aussies! Come on!' but not quite with the same gusto as before. The car bumper stickers announce: White Australia has a Black History. A new, brooding, depressive and self-critical phase has been ushered in, to replace the manic hype of our former nationalistic fervour. Abroad, in the United States or in Asia, Australians still seem brash, confident, assertive, even boastful, but this is largely an outward and worn persona, which fails to do justice to the new cultural attitude.

Australians are engaged in a further psychological descent, and in an heroic, ego-based Western society 'descent' is always resisted and denied. Australians try to make light of their own dilemmas: we are suffering from an ongoing identity-crisis that we must decide to overcome, announce the newspaper editorials, almost as if our present crisis could be resolved by an act of will. Our slump, both moral and socio-economic, is seen as 'typical' of a young country on the verge of breaking constitutional ties with parental Britain and embarking on a new phase as a republic. Other commentators take a different line: Australians are actually crippled by the self-loathing and guilt arising from their historical mistreatment of Aboriginals. These political, social, and racial points of view all have a good deal of validity and in their own contexts are true enough. But we can also explore the contemporary unsettlement of Australia through an archetypal perspective and read this cultural depression as a psychological crisis.

As indicated in the previous chapter, white Australian consciousness is only superficially part of the Australian scene, and only apparently linked with the Aboriginal earth upon which it lives and moves. There is in fact a considerable chasm between society and nature—a chasm that can be further conceptualised as a psychological gap between consciousness and the unconscious. White consciousness here is largely defensive and heavily armoured: the landscape is seen as threatening and malign, and the job of 'heroic' white society has been to deny the strangeness of the place and to pretend that we are actually back in Britain. In Australian cultural experience the landscape is coterminous with the unconscious: it is vast, ancient, mythological, and wholly other. We have denied the true spirit of the land, and its indigenous inhabitants, for two hundred years of white settlement, and now the repressed is coming back to haunt us. We are not just caught up in what is popularly dismissed as 'white guilt': the Western ego senses, or feels, that it is not entirely authentic, and that its former pretence at integrity and belonging are no longer adequate. White Australians do indeed have a black history, but that black history is now the urgent and demanding psychological present.

No-one likes to be told, not even by a well-meaning therapist, that depression is good for them. But in Australian society a bout of depression is precisely what is required in order to lower the threshold of consciousness and to organically link it with the deep unconscious. Only from this psychocultural depression can the essential connections be made that will revivify the nation and restore integrity and self-regard to its citizens. We are dissolving slowly into landscape, but it is a necessary dissolution that ought not be resisted or willed away by resorting to the outworn heroics of the past. We are experiencing what Freud might call a regression for the sake of advancement.

When the ego-personality is spurious or false, the unconscious will most often present itself as a devouring maw that seems to undermine, threaten, and endanger consciousness. In Australian literature and popular culture, we find countless images of landscape as an archetypal field that would destroy the white intruders. We wage an ongoing war against the natural elements, against bushfires, drought, floods, winds. In the nineteenth century, the classic motif in Australian stories was that of the young and helpless child lost in the bush: nature was a malevolent force claiming human lives for itself. What took place in Australian culture was the reverse of English Romanticism: 'Mother Nature' did not attend and care for her children, but rather the Terrible Mother of mythological imagination tended to impress itself upon our experience of the earth and the natural elements.

In some Australian writing, nature is anthro-pomorphically portrayed as a demonic primordial lover, whose erotic embrace leads to death and disintegration. In Barcroft Boake's 'Where the Dead Men Lie' (1897), the 'Earth's loved sons' find that their bond with mother nature leads to the 'endless tryst' of death. In the Proem to Henry

Handel Richardson's *Australia Felix* (1917), nature is mythologised as a sorceress who 'held captive, without chains' those who had 'so lightly invaded [this] ancient country'. Nature is imaged as a

> primeval monster in the sun, her breasts freely bared, [watching] with a malignant eye the efforts made by these puny mortals to tear their lips away.[2]

Even though our adolescent spirit may be crushed by such a force, a genuine relationship with nature and the primal earth must be forged. This is the great challenge confronting Australian consciousness. Living behind masculinist barriers and rational defences is only a half-life. Anyway, these barriers seem to be falling down now of their own accord, and we will be forced sooner or later into a new encounter with the unconscious and the unknown. We can only hope that our spirit will not be completely disintegrated by this encounter. Or maybe, as so much Australian culture attests, our particular kind of masculinist-defensive spirit will *have* to be sacrificed to nature. Perhaps only then a new kind of human spirit, more connected with this country and not imposed upon it by a colonialist-imperial order, will emerge, Phoenix-like, from the death of the old.

Lacking an organic connection to the earth beneath it, Australia can appear shadowy, unreal, lifeless. In 1922 D.H. Lawrence wrote: 'There was the vast town of Sydney. And it didn't seem to be real, it seemed to be sprinkled on the surface of a darkness into which it never penetrated'.[3] In 1939 Patrick White noted that Australian society and nature were completely at odds: 'The country existed in spite of the town. It was not aware of it. There was no connecting link'. White compared Australian society with 'an ugly scab on the body of the earth'. 'It was so ephemeral. Some day it would drop off, leaving a pink, clean place underneath.'[4]

This hideous image was used in the same year by A.D. Hope, who wrote, in his poem 'Australia':

> And her five cities, like five teeming sores,
> Each drains her, a vast parasite robber-state
> Where second-hand Europeans pullulate
> Timidly on the edge of alien shores.[5]

These are intensely disturbing, deliberately shocking images of society, a testimony to the emotional impact of our cultural dissociation upon creative writers.

The problem of unconscious and involuntary sacrifice

To be suspended above the ground invites disaster and ruin. An unsupported social structure is forever precarious, and in our literature we find images of society poised over a dreadful abyss. The opening image of Richardson's ironically titled *Australia Felix* is of a digger on the Victorian goldfields falling headlong to his death in a deep gravel pit:

> The digger fell forward on his face ... nose and mouth pressed into the sticky mud as into a mask; and over his defenceless body, with a roar that burst his ear-drums, broke stupendous masses of earth.[6]

Here we have a memorable representation of the human spirit's fatal 'marriage' with the earth in death. An eerie, mythic quality is found in the image of the death-mask, reminding us of the earthen masks or personae worn in ancient festivals. This digger's experiences symbolise what could be a modern Australian symbolic rite: the transformation of spirit suspended arrogantly above earth, to spirit suddenly crushed by earth and wedded to it. It is interesting that the moment he becomes 'defenceless'—the moment he loses his human mask—he is made to take on the sticky earthen mask supplied by nature. In other words, as soon as we fall out of our normal workaday persona, nature is ready to supply us with a mask of her own. Nature, disturbed at being shunned by our arrogant spirit, is quick to immobilise and petrify the 'puny mortals'.

In historical fact, many of our early explorers were conquered by the land, and they found that, when the second-hand 'European' colonial settlements were left behind, nature seemed keen to dissolve them. This is especially the experience found in Patrick White's *Voss* (1957),[7] whose central character is based in part upon the historical figures of Leichhardt and Eyre. The newly arrived German explorer was appalled at the way Australians 'huddled' together in coastal settlements, apparently denying the grandeur and magnificence of the land. But although Voss set out to 'conquer' the land, in fact it quickly conquered him, and his journey into death and disintegration was presided over, and seemingly inspired by, a mythological demon-lover or seductive enchantress. White's novel appears to show that Australians 'huddle' defensively from elemental nature for good reason, and that to embrace nature in Australia is indeed to become one of the Earth's ill-fated 'loved sons'.

Randolph Stow's poem 'The Singing Bones' explores this theme with acute sensitivity and insight. He sees the seductiveness of death-by-nature in Australia, and argues that the explorers Leichhardt and Gibson, and 'Lawson's tramps', were 'by choice made mummia and air'. There is something in the Australian psyche that predisposes the human personality to go off the rails, to abort reality, to turn renegade and become dissolved into landscape. We huddle and cling to the persona, the surface, the coastline, because the urge to run amok is so powerful and strong. Stow deftly psychologises the forbidding terrain:

Out there their place is, where the charts are gapped,
unreachable, unmapped, and mainly in the mind.[8]

The natural world is *without* and yet also *within*. The 'nature' that claims lives is not only the remote outback, but the remote places in the Australian unconscious. Is it the Australian unconscious or the landscape that is peculiarly vicious and malign? Or is it, as I suspect, that the *distance* between spirit and nature, conscious and unconscious, has a destructive and enervating effect on human life? When there is no organic connection between spirit and earth, earth rips spirit out of its human context and gives it an earthen death-mask. If Australians do not build a connection between mind and earth in life, a connection will be forced upon them destructively, in death. Those who 'die of landscape' (Stow) are involved in a kind of negative or unconscious cultural sacrifice.

Poet Judith Wright first understood these deaths-by-landscape in meaningful cultural terms. In her 1961 essay, 'The Upside-down Hut', she wrote:

> Are all these dead men in our literature, then, a kind of ritual sacrifice? And just what is being sacrificed? Is it perhaps the European consciousness—dominating, puritanical, analytical (Richard Mahony was a doctor, Voss a botanist), that Lawrence saw as negated by this landscape? ... Reconciliation, then, is a matter of death—the death of the European mind, its absorption into the soil it has struggled against.[9]

This country clearly needs a new kind of spirit, one that cultural development will surely bring to birth. It may still be too early to know what the new spirit will be like. Meanwhile, the destruction of the old—the 'European consciousness' as Wright puts it—continues. The problem is that all this takes place completely unconsciously. Australian social consciousness—so rational, so busy, commitedly secular—knows very little about the religious or sacramental process taking place within its own depths. All the signs are there in our literary culture, but the *images* of this psychocultural sacrifice have not yet been translated into *concepts* that would enable us to understand the situation better. We have only poetry, hints, images, to go by. We refuse to sacrifice something of ourselves *knowingly* to the land and to the deep unconscious, but the sacrifices take place anyway, whether or not we are aware of them. Our ritual offerings are enacted involuntarily, as if in a trance or dream.

There is plenty of sacramental awareness when the Other that claims lives is a known, public enemy. Witness the enormous amount of national feeling and sentiment invested in Australian war experiences, especially the Gallipoli campaign, which was a bloody near-massacre of Australian soldiers. We readily revere those lives lost in sacramental terms and erect public monuments 'lest we forget' the human cost. The First World War inspired enormous community commitment and support because it actually tapped into Australia's unconscious sacrificial compulsion. Men, boys, women felt the call of the country and responded accordingly with great courage. We are good at that kind of sacrifice; but bloody, physical deaths against a human foe are not what the Australian psyche needs. What is needed is far more subtle, more psychologically (rather than militaristically) demanding, and more concerned with this land than with the Dardanelles. The danger to ourselves and to the world is that until we understand what is required in this country the sacrificial impulse will continue to be projected in exotic, foreign parts and released in military activity and theatres of war.

A common theme in fairytales is that of a country beset by a sacrifice-demanding monster or dragon who lives in the dark woods or just beyond the settled areas. The monster has a voracious appetite and keeps demanding human and animal sacrifices, lest he destroy the entire known world. The country lives in constant fear and is gradually depleted and reduced by the monster's demands. Jungian psychology would argue that the ruling consciousness, sometimes personified by the king or ruler, has become separated from an instinctual, archetypal source, which has grown 'monstrous' through neglect and repression. This neglected element draws more and more psychic energy to itself, eventually threatening the stability and economy of consciousness. In the tales, usually the only way to stop this intolerable situation is by heroic activity (slaying the monster), or by creating a dialogue with the monster and finding out how to satisfy its needs in other ways. Until wisdom or 'right action' intervenes—often personified by a seer, monk, knight, or oracle—the demon-monster continues to consume innocent lives. This is where Australian society is still caught in archetypal terms: it is still feeding the demonic hunger of the unconscious psyche; it exists prior to heroic activity or conscious intervention. We have not yet graduated to the point where spirit attempts a dialogue with the devouring unconscious. We have not asked the sacrificial compulsion what it wants.

Earth-sacrifice in popular culture

A chilling example of our unconscious compulsion to sacrifice to the elemental earth is the well-known folk-tale *Picnic at Hanging Rock*. Joan Lindsay's novel (1967),[10] and the internationally successful film by Peter Weir (1975),[11] depict the uncanny and awful earth-sacrifice of beautiful young women at the archaic and craggy monument that is Hanging Rock. This rock, we are told, erupted from the earth's interior millions of years ago. One of the girls, Irma, says in a trance-like tone: 'It has been waiting a million years, just for us'. No resistance is evident as she is drawn by almost occult attraction toward the rock; nor is there any resistance evident from the similarly enchanted Miranda, the central figure in this bizarre ritual of human sacrifice. The dominant impression of the so-called picnic is one of trance-like unconscious ritual, or acting as if caught in a dream. In the film, the haunting special effects, the sound of cicadas and other insects, the stylised symbolic photography, and the sound-track of the deeply resonant organ with shrill notes of the Pan-flute, all combine to create a stunning atmosphere of dream, myth, and ritual.

Lindsay has performed an important cultural task in showing us how unconscious, entranced, and subservient to archetypal forces we are in Australia. In our national anthem we say that we are 'young and free', thinking we act by our own volition, but the unacknowledged archetypal processes simply grab us from behind, where they perform their lethal enactment of symbolic activities. The schoolgirls of Appleyard College are led to their destruction on the face of the rock because their human society is asleep.

Similarly, in recent history and popular culture, we have the tragic case of Azaria Chamberlain (1980–1980), narrated now in numerous texts,[12] and portrayed in the American film *Evil Angels* (1988).[13] While the Chamberlain family camped beside Uluru (Ayers Rock), baby Azaria, only a few weeks old, was seized at night by a dingo and dragged off to her death. The raw, elemental, and archetypal nature of this tragic incident immediately gripped the nation: the innocent (sleeping) human being is destroyed by nature, by a wild dog; and, as in *Picnic*, the event takes place at a great and mysterious earth-monument, Uluru, a place long associated with Aboriginal ceremonies and rites of passage. And, as in *Picnic*, no bodily or other remains were discovered after the tragic disappearance, adding to the mystery and enigma of the case.

The unconscious cultural need to offer an earth-sacrifice was strongly activated by this incident. As with any unconscious psychic process, the contents of the symbolic drama are negatively literalised and personified. Rumours flash across the country that the name Azaria means 'sacrifice in the wilderness'. There are further rumours of devil worshippers and ritual murderers in central Australia and Queensland, and the Chamberlains are felt to belong to this occult group. But it is the mother, Lindy, who becomes the carrier of the image of the death-dealing maternal earth, the womb-matrix that devours its own offspring. She murdered Azaria, the nation announces, eager to literalise and even more eager to find a scapegoat. Even a court of law finds her guilty on almost no real evidence: indeed, what was at that time called *evidence* was later revealed to be wholly without foundation. These events can be viewed as a sort of national psychosis, an eruption of irrationality and outrage, with the powerful image of earth-sacrifice at the centre. Lindy Chamberlain was victimised, jailed, and martyred by a supposedly egalitarian, fair-minded, secular Australia, because our society cannot attend to its own unconscious sacred imperatives, cannot atone for its own distance from the earth and the archetypal *other*.

Australian settlers unsettled

We do not require literal killings or Aztec-like human sacrifices, but a letting of psychic blood, an offering of some inner part of ourselves to place. A dialogue is needed, both with the land and with the Aboriginal people, who are themselves the symbolic continuum of the landscape, in the sense that they are wedded emotionally and spiritually with the land. A conquering people, we are not particularly good at initiating dialogue. Judith Wright once again was one of the first to explore this complex problem. She noted how conquerors expect everything to go their way: we can plunder, rape, and pillage, all in the name of development and civilisation, but we do not know how to give back to the land, how to forge a spiritual connection with it. This is because we do not know, nor do we *want* to know, how to sacrifice to our own inner depths, to the nature within ourselves. Always these twin levels of inner and outer reality spiral together. It is oftentimes difficult, as Wright's poetry attests, to differentiate what we need to do on behalf of 'landscape' from what we need to do for the sake of the elemental psyche within each of us.

The spiritual inadequacy of Australian society is the subject of much of Wright's poetry, especially her later work. Although we have prospered physically and materially on this land, more subtle realities, such as our psychical relation to place, which would grant full admission to a country and fellowship with it, are denied us as conquerors:

> The blue crane fishing in Cooloolah's twilight
> has fished there longer than our centuries.
> He is the certain heir of lake and evening,
> and he will wear their colour till he dies;
>
> but I'm a stranger, come of a conquering people.
> I cannot share his calm, who watch his lake,
> being unloved by all my eyes delight in
> and made uneasy, for an old murder's sake.
>
> Those dark-skinned people who once named Cooloolah
> knew that no land is lost or won by wars
> for earth is spirit; the invader's feet will tangle
> in nets there and his blood be thinned by fears.[14]

Conquerors of new lands are themselves eventually conquered by the land, because internally they are racked by self-doubt, plagued by fears, tortured by personal inadequacies. The natural world within and without seems to turn against them. Their acts of hubris constellate the same consequences hubris in ancient classic drama brought: the vengeance of nature and the perishing of the soul. Conquerors of land can find no ultimate solace or fulfilment, no deep satisfaction, if they do not embrace the spirit of *place*, allowing themselves to connect spiritually, organically, to the world around them. We cannot live a full life shut up inside the sterile, rational confines of the ego. Sooner or later, we must break out of this cocoon and risk the encounter with nature. Wright breaks out of our cocoon and finds that, to her horror, nature will not or does not embrace her. Some commentators have said that nature in Australia is inherently harsh, and therefore cannot offer any expected romantic experiences. 'In Australian writing Nature endures, rather than protects or nourishes.'[15] But Wright's vision goes deeper than this romantic complaint about nature as unmotherly. She understands how, after allowing ourselves to lose our vital connection with nature, we have made nature appear indifferent or malign. We cannot psychically and physically abuse nature on a grand scale and then expect it to nurture and protect us.

In 'Eroded Hills', Wright argues that we have not only injured our spiritual pact with nature, but even our biological link with the fruits of the earth has been disrupted:

These hills my father's father stripped;
and, beggars to the winter wind,
they crouch like shoulders naked and whipped—
humble, abandoned, out of mind.

Of their scant creeks I drank once
and ate sour cherries from old trees
found in their gullies fruiting by chance.
Neither fruit nor water gave my mind ease.[16]

Wright's poem is not simply a protest against patriarchal abuse of landscape, nor can it be categorised (in that deradicalising way so often found in commentaries on her work) as a poem about 'conservation'. It is a poem about the withheld love of nature, about the chasm that exists between the primal earth and the sterile consciousness of white society. Wright is showing the spiritual legacy of a conquering society, which achieves a great deal in external terms, but which has no sustaining internal link to the biopsychical (human and nonhuman) life of nature.

Because of this deep disjunction, Australians remain anxious, restless, unsure of themselves. The widespread search for identity in Australia is not merely an intellectual or cognitive one that ends when we arrive at comforting national images or consensual conventions about who the 'real Australians' are. Identity cannot be achieved in this pre-programmed way but must arise from within. When society and nature, conscious and unconscious, are organically related (as seems to be the case in most indigenous cultures) there is no more talk about the problem of identity; the emotional depths of existence are filled and a sense of character or personality is assured. 'Alienation and rootlessness,' writes Jung, 'are the dangers that lie in wait for the conqueror of foreign lands.'[17]

It is important to realise that the nationalist temperament governed Wright's early work, when her aim was to affirm and celebrate the supposed 'oneness' with the land that the early pioneers and settlers had achieved for future generations. In poems such as 'Bullocky', 'Remittance Man', 'South of My Days', and 'For New England', she celebrates early Australian experience by turning ordinary settlers and pioneers into figures of legend. These poems (all from the 1946 collection) were pro-establishment and condoned the pioneering mentality: good honest toil builds culture and masculinist effort provides a solid foundation for Australian society. The legendary Bullocky is felt to open up the land, to tame a wild landscape, and to make over the country in the likeness of humanity. His efforts render the land sweet and productive:

> O vine, grow close upon that bone
> and hold it with your rooted hand.
> The prophet Moses feeds the grape,
> and fruitful is the Promised Land.[18]

But by the time we get to 'Eroded Hills' (1953) and 'At Cooloolah' (1955) Wright's Australian landscape is vastly different. No more does a sweet and fruitful earth bear witness to a happy alliance between nature and human progress; now the earth is scorched and abused, and nature and humanity are torn apart. The nationalist myth of the pioneering pact with the land has given way to a contemporary myth of alienation and rootlessness.

Judith Wright's long career models the crucial psychic changes that Australian culture will have to undergo. When first setting forth upon new land, it is important that the colonising society believe in its own progress and development, and imagine that simple honest toil is creating authentic culture. However, postcolonial generations must reconsider this view, acknowledging that social consolidation has occurred at the expense of the indigenous world. The artist's eye, appalled by the shocking gap between society, psyche, and nature, now exposes the old nationalist order as a sham and pretence. Nationalists accuse Wright of becoming anti-Australian, whereas she has really moved with the currents of the Australian psyche itself, shifting to a more profound, if much less flattering, psychocultural position.

Australian settlers have to feel *unsettled*; that is the beginning of our maturation process and the seed of real cultural wisdom. It is only by feeling unsettled that we begin to feel the psychic gap between society and nature, between our rational conscious attitudes and our more elemental unconscious forces. The more we become aware of the gap, the narrower it becomes. Feeling unsettled, unauthentic, doubtful—this is a form of cultural suffering and a *conscious* sacrifice of the ego's unimpeded growth and happy development. The contemporary 'unsettlement' of Australia, wrongly dismissed as a white guilt trip or trivialised as a simple identity crisis, is a way of consciously and intentionally connecting with the elemental dimension that has been maligned, repressed, and kept 'out of mind' (Wright).

On the art of sacrifice, the Aboriginal culture has much to teach white Australia. Aboriginal people have long been aware that in order to maintain an equilibrium between the human and nonhuman worlds, sacrifices must be made to the elemental earth to ensure that humanity remains in harmony with the cosmos. If humanity forgets to pay due homage to the archetypal forces and loses an attitude of humility toward the cosmos, everything would go awry and the world would fall into chaos. There is a memorable moment in Bruce Chatwin's *The Songlines*, where the conflict between Euro-Australian attitudes and Aboriginal practices is poignantly revealed:

> The Aboriginals ... never understood why the missionaries forbade their innocent sacrifices. They slaughtered no victims, animal or human. Instead, when they wished to thank the earth for its gifts, they would simply slit a vein in their forearms and let their own blood spatter the ground.
>
> 'Not a heavy price to pay,' he [Arkady] said. 'The wars of the twentieth century are the price for having taken too much.'[19]

This is my own position precisely. If the Western ego can achieve some degree of humility toward the greater cosmic forces, then it finds its proper place in the order of things. If it does not honour the need for sacrifice, then the innate sacrificial impulse becomes compulsive and unconscious, whence it enacts a terrible toll. The more conscious our sacrifice can be, the less likely we are to fall victim to the sacrificial impulse gone mad.

4

On not crossing the gap

D.H. Lawrence saw non-Aboriginal Australians perched arrogantly, if rootlessly, upon ancient, archaic, sacred ground. He was wryly amused, when he visited here in the 1920s, by the contrast between the confidently secular, busy, yet spiritually hollow people and the still, silent, yet spiritually powerful landscape. He felt that Australian society was unreal, that it was not an organic thing but that it hung as it were in mid-air, above the earth:

> There was the vast town of Sydney. And it didn't seem to be real, it seemed to be sprinkled on the surface of a darkness into which it never penetrated.[1]

Elsewhere in *Kangaroo* (1923) he writes that, after dark, the spurious white society seemed to disappear into a void as the primal landscape reasserted itself:

> As soon as night came, all the raggle-taggle of amorphous white settlements disappeared, and the continent of the kangaroo reassumed its strange, unvisited glamour, a kind of virgin sensual aloofness.
> (p. 30)

Lawrence's great theme in all his writings, regardless of their geographical setting, was the rootlessness and alienation of modern man. For Lawrence, humanity had attempted, in its intellectual arrogance and hubris, to cut itself off from nature and primal instinct. He felt, as did

Freud and Jung, that consciousness had dangerously disengaged itself from the deep unconscious, and that it lacked any compensatory or grounding connection to the vital, life-sustaining world below the conscious mind. Western culture, for modernist writers and thinkers, had turned into T.S. Eliot's 'unreal city' by virtue of its denial of the archaic, passional ground of human existence. Lawrence, as detractors of his Australian novels have pointed out,[2] seized upon the evident discontinuity between Australian society and landscape in order to add further dimension to his own universal theme. However, the universality of this theme does not detract in any way from its local, and specifically Australian, significance. Far from imposing his vision artificially and externally upon the Australian scene, as some have asserted, it has always seemed to me that Lawrence understood Australia and Australians, from within, despite his brief visit here. He was no mere tourist, but a writer of acute sensibility and intuition, who could rapidly gain a personal understanding of the spirit of the place in which he was living.

The absence of vital energy

For Lawrence, human society is nourished and fed by two sources: the spirit of nature (vital energy) and the spirit of culture (tradition). White Australian society, he argues in *Kangaroo* and in *The Boy in the Bush* (1924), has little or no access to either source. Australia has been unable to import its spirit from its European origins. Despite what Australian Church leaders and promoters of high culture have believed, the spirit of culture and religion is not especially transportable or moveable. We have the outward trappings of European civilisation here, but the essence of it did not quite survive the journey. To Lawrence, Australian society seemed like an uninspired imitation or replica of life lived elsewhere:

Even the heart of Sydney itself—an imitation of London
and New York—without any core or pith of meaning.
Business going on full speed: but only because it is the
other end of English and American business.

The absence of any inner meaning: and at the same
time the great sense of vacant spaces.
(*Kangaroo*, p. 24)

He went on to say that the 'inside soul' of Euro-Australians
'just withers and goes into the outside, and they're all just
lusty robust hollow stalks of people' (p. 143). As if to
compensate for this felt hollowness, Australians seemed to
Lawrence to be hell-bent on the pursuit of material wealth
and consumer goods. Australians want more and more
money and material security, as if transferring their desire
for 'more' life and spiritual substance into material terms.
But for Lawrence, 'even the rush for money has no real pip
in it':

When all is said and done, even money is not much
good where there is no genuine culture. Money is a
means to rising to a higher, subtler, fuller state of
consciousness, or nothing. (*Kangaroo*, p. 25)

The other source for spiritual nourishment is from
'below', not from the 'higher' world of religion, tradition,
and culture, but from the lower world of nature, vital
energy, and the earth. If we are unable to tap the higher
sources of the Christian spirit (which for Lawrence had
dried up in Europe itself), there is also the darker, pagan,
chthonic spirit of nature. But the inorganic, artificial
character of Australian society makes it difficult to draw
anything from the earth beneath it or from the natural
world around it. This, nevertheless, was the spiritual source
that Australians would have to learn to tap, however
problematical their current spiritual and psychosocial
situation.

The untouchable earth

A further complication arises: the land itself, the aboriginal spirit of place, resists the society that has been foisted upon it. Not only are Euro-Australians unrelated to the land by their own doing, but they are spiritually shunned by the new-old land. Most Australians, Lawrence felt, are unaware of this deeper alienation or exclusion, but they would have to become aware of it in their ultimate quest for national identity and spiritual maturity. Lawrence continually commented on the 'strange *unvisited* glamour' and on the 'virgin sensual *aloofness*' of the landscape. In archetypal terms, Australia is constructed in ways reminiscent of the Greek deity Artemis, who was virginal, wild, untouchable, remote, steely, and resistant to the advances of men. Except that Australia is not youthful like Artemis, but archaic and old, like a virginal or untouched crone. A.D. Hope describes this double kore/crone aspect well when he writes of the land as 'a breast / still tender but within the womb is dry'.

In *Kangaroo* Lawrence's fictional persona Richard Somers announces: 'This land always gives me the feeling that it doesn't *want* to be touched, it doesn't *want* men to get hold of it' (p. 323). In *The Boy in the Bush* Jack Grant declares that 'Nobody could actually *belong* to the country' (p. 8).[3] Lawrence was aware, as Judith Wright became aware after him, that the conqueror of foreign ground cannot fully or finally conquer the *spirit* of the place that has been appropriated in political and material terms. At this deeper level the conqueror remains the outsider, and the spiritual curse upon the invader-conqueror is that they will never *feel* at home or at peace in the stolen territory. They will be plagued, as Jack Grant puts it, by the 'feeling of remote unreality' (p. 8). The obsessional pursuit of identity by many Australians, both before but especially after Lawrence's visit, is symptomatic of this cultural unease and spiritual malaise, and no nationalist program or intellectual formula will put an end to the restless search until the *spiritual* basis of the problem is confronted.

Death by landscape

Lawrence responded with ambivalence to the spiritual otherness of Australia. On the one hand he found it exhilarating, exotic, primeval. On the other hand he found it threatening, disintegrative, overwhelmingly 'other'. This ambivalence runs throughout both his Australian novels:

> The distances were clear and mellow and beautiful,
> but soulless, and nobody alive in the world. The silent,
> lonely gruesomeness of Australia gave Jack the blues.
> (*Boy*, p. 70)

> And the vast, uninhabited land frightened him. It
> seemed so hoary and lost, so unapproachable.
> (*Kangaroo*, p. 9)

What I wish to emphasise is that Lawrence's characters, and Lawrence himself, felt and suffered from the spiritual alienation that is the subject of the Australian novels. It is not at all the case that Lawrence represented Australians as blind or ignorant victims of a spiritual malaise wholly of their own making. Australians are confronted by an inherently difficult psychospiritual situation, and Lawrence has no simple solution to present us.

Somers describes a moment of terror in the Western Australian landscape, which causes him to flee from those environs in a state of panic. (This fictional account is entirely autobiographical, as we learn from Lawrence's letter to Katherine Susannah Prichard.)[4]

> It was so phantom-like, so ghostly, with its tall pale
> trees and many dead trees, like corpses, partly charred
> by bush fires: and then the foliage so dark, like grey-
> green iron. And then it was so deathly still. Even the

few birds seemed to be swamped in silence ... He
walked on, had walked a mile or so into the bush, and
had just come to a clump of tall, nude, dead trees,
shining almost phosphorescent with the moon, when
the terror of the bush overcame him ... There was
something among the trees, and his hair began to stir
with terror, on his head. There was a presence.
(*Kangaroo*, p. 9)

It is too easy for intellectual readers to laugh dismissively at
Lawrence's encounter with the spirit of place. It is, for a
start, extremely difficult to present an experience such as
this in fictional terms. How to capture the sense of a
remote, 'hoary', indifferent spirit of place without seeming
to present this 'presence' as a sort of literal ghost, or as a
supernatural force, or a swamp-dwelling Bunyip? How to
be true to one's intuitive feeling in the bush without creating
ludicrous melodrama or an implausible 'close encounter'?
Still, plausible or not, Lawrence strove to present the
ambivalent nature of *his* encounter with the Australian 'spirit
of place' (p. 10). To fully experience Australian landscape,
not merely to look at it as a tourist, but to experience its
psychic atmosphere as a sensitive artist, is for Lawrence to
encounter something strangely alien, something distantly
remote and almost non- or even anti-human.

There is an enormous psychic gap between the
consciousness of Europeans and the primal reality of
Australian landscape. The gap is so great that
consciousness could be swallowed up if it attempted to
cross the gap in search of psychic roots in the local soil.
Australian literature is full of many examples of the fate of
those 'poor wretched souls' (as Lawson calls them) who fall
into the gap and who become psychically and/or physically
overwhelmed by place. Literary scholars can always find
logical reasons for why these numerous characters go mad

or disintegrate: it is said that they suffer from loneliness and human deprivation, from extreme isolation, from depression and melancholia, from 'bush-madness'. But the poet Randolph Stow gets it right when he says that such figures 'die of landscape'.[5] Or in my own language, they fall into the yawning gap that separates consciousness and society from the aboriginal spirit of place. They suffer such an onslaught from the primordial unconscious that the over-civilised and inorganic European consciousness is disintegrated. European consciousness has not, because of its long and slow development in European soil and its relative independence from the lower depths of the unconscious, been exposed to such archaic levels for some time. Lawrence felt that the Australian spirit of place was 'too far back' and that he could 'not reach so awfully far'. There is a great risk involved in crossing that gap, and Lawrence felt he was not, as artist or as man, equal to the task.

But the Euro-Australians who live here will have to risk the encounter. Robust poets such as Neilson, Judith Wright, and Les Murray have accepted the challenge and survived; more than survived, they have flourished. For once the archaic spirit of the continent is contacted it can act, not only as a force of disintegration, but as A.D. Hope knew, as a 'savage and scarlet' spirit that is capable of bringing a profound psychical rebirth, a deepening, and regeneration. And it is as 'savage and scarlet as no green hills dare';[6] in other words, it brings about a profound and primordial awakening that is not possible in the cultivated and developed mental climate of Europe. One has to dig too far down into European soil to find a similar, or equal, level of primordiality.[7] It is Australia, not Britain, that will give rise to a future profound awakening of the indwelling spirit. Lawrence knew this, and although he felt 'glad to have glimpsed it',[8] he did not feel mentally or physically strong enough to participate in it himself.

The Australian dilemma: sacrifice or be sacrificed

Lawrence knew that a rapprochement with the spirit of place would necessitate real sacrifice:

> 'It always seems to me,' said Somers, 'that somebody will have to water Australia with their blood before it's a real man's country. The soil, the very plants seem to be waiting for it.' (*Kangaroo*, p. 85)

This is a controversial and much-discussed passage, which often seems to me to be misunderstood by Australian readers. Lawrence is not necessarily providing a rationale for ritual blood-sacrifices to the earth, either at Uluru, Hanging Rock, or elsewhere. He is speaking metaphorically, poetically, and mythologically about the sacrifice that is required before real contact with the spirit of place is possible. 'Blood' is a key Lawrentian symbol, and it generally means psychic energy, libido, the pulse of life. Something primal, red, and living in us will have to be offered to the earth before we can connect with its 'savage and scarlet' spirit. Like must meet with like, and we will have to reach down into ourselves to find something that is parallel to what we have to come to terms with. An encounter with the spirit of place is at once an encounter with our own lower depths; it necessitates a descent or *nekyia* into the psychic underworld to find there the red primordial wellspring which can 'meet' the genius of this country and heal the dissociation between society and nature.

From this perspective, the sacrifice required of Euro-Australians is the sacrifice of their obsessive attachment to what Lawrence calls 'cerebral' or 'mental consciousness'.[9] The contact with lower depths requires a certain psychic fluidity, a shift in human identity and a loosening of the tie to the rational and conscious mind. Not that the rational mind itself has to be sacrificed. Lawrence would have none of that, but would regard this as cultural regression. It is simply the *attachment* to the rational mind that has to be sacrificed (in a sense, a very Buddhist idea), so that a psychic journey and a deepening can begin, both for the individual and for Australian society as a whole. The rational mind and the ego have to remain intact as we deepen our lives and our culture in the direction of the dark primal ground. If ego-consciousness is not respected and maintained, then we fall into the gap because we are no longer grounded in social reality. We then become what Lawrence elsewhere calls 'primitivists' and 'cultural renegades'.[10] Ironically, Lawrence himself is constructed as primitivist and renegade by those who fail to appreciate that he advocated not only a descent to the unconscious but also a maintaining of social and worldly consciousness. As I have already indicated, Lawrence chose not to conduct his own descent here, but opted for New and Old Mexico, and various parts of Europe, to be the locus of his own psychic journeying.

If Australians will not sacrifice for the sake of psychic deepening, they will perforce *be sacrificed* to a deepening gone wrong. This is Lawrence's chilling and cautionary warning to Euro-Australian society. If we do not voluntarily attempt to explore the psychic underworld, we will be involuntarily dragged into it, with destructive and negative consequences.

> What was the good of trying to be an alert conscious man here? You couldn't. Drift, drift into a sort of obscurity, backwards into a nameless past, hoary as the country is hoary. Strange old feelings wake in the soul: old, non-human feelings. And an old, old indifference, like a torpor, invades the spirit.
> (*Kangaroo*, p. 204)

If Australians remain unaware of their need to make a spiritual adjustment to the land, the place itself will act like a lead weight upon consciousness, drawing it into inertia, indifference, and inactivity. This is what psychologist Ronald Conway calls the 'Great Australian Stupor', and Conway's insights have, in turn, been influenced by Lawrence's writings.[11] When Australians boast about their easy, relaxed, tensionless life-style 'down under', they may well be celebrating their regression into a pre-conscious or twilight state. This is also why Lawrence felt uneasy about Australian anti-intellectualism. On the face of it, Lawrence was himself 'anti-intellectual', advocating a return to eros and to 'blood consciousness'. But he was worried by the lack of awareness with which Euro-Australians seemed to pursue their downward course. Lawrence wanted to see tension, nervous tension, between the longing for the psychic depths and the desire for a fully alert, adult, and mature consciousness. This was his own paradoxical position, which in many ways resembles Jung's concept of individuation as a pathway between the psychic opposites, between the demands of the primal unconscious and the duties and claims of consciousness.[12]

Lawrence puts the vital question to Euro-Australian culture and society:

> Would the people waken this ancient land, or would the land put them to sleep, drift them back into the torpid semi-consciousness of the world of the twilight? (*Kangaroo*, p. 204)

Will we have in Australia an unconscious regression to the ancient past, to inactivity and mental stupor? Or will we make a *conscious connection* with the 'savage and scarlet' spirit of place and waken both ourselves and it in a new era of spiritual and cultural development? Lawrence got out of Australia, and so it is hard to see his actions as a vote of confidence for the possibility of spiritual regeneration. Still, we have the evidence of contemporary Australian poetry

(Wright and Murray) and recent fiction (Malouf, Jolley, Murnane, among others) to support the view that regeneration is possible and that the construction of a new, deeper, more profound consciousness is already under way.

Bailing out

In *Kangaroo* Richard Somers feels the great Australian earth drawing him toward it with almost magnetic power. And he is, like Lawrence, at odds with himself. Intellectually he wants to 'give in' to Australia, but emotionally he feels unable or unwilling to make the descent that is required. Hence he is plagued by negative and morbid symptoms: 'he felt the torpor coming over him' (p. 204); he thinks his mind is 'melting away' (p. 390), that he is being Australianised 'in his sleep' (p. 166). Somers puts his contrary feelings and impulses to his Welsh friend in New South Wales:

> 'I love it, Jaz. I don't love people. But this place—it goes into my marrow, and makes me feel drunk. I love Australia … [It] tempts me … [but] I don't want to give in to the place. It's too strong. It would lure me quite away from myself … It's too tempting. It's too big a stride, Jaz.' (pp. 405–06)

The similarity between the fictional Somers and Lawrence himself is strikingly revealed in a letter Lawrence wrote to the Australian Katherine Susannah Prichard,[13] in which he tried to explain to this passionately nationalist writer why he could not remain in Australia.

> Don't imagine either that I am bolting as fast as all that from Australia. We're not going till August 10th— and three months in one place isn't so bad. For some things too I love Australia: its weird, far-away natural beauty and its remote, almost coal-age pristine quality. Only it's too far for me. I can't reach so awfully far. Further than Egypt. I feel I slither on the edge of a

> gulf, reaching to grasp its atmosphere and spirit. It
> eludes me, and always would. It is too far back ...
> strains my heart, reaching. But I am very glad to have
> glimpsed it.

For Lawrence, with his consumptive condition and frail
body, the gulf between his own consciousness and the
Australian spirit of place may indeed have been 'too far'. He
did not want to risk linking his own genius with our *genius
loci*. Even in the different atmosphere of North America,
and later back in 'over-upholstered Europe' (p. 175), he only
lived for another eight years before dying of tuberculosis.
But we need not begrudge Lawrence his right to bail out, or
abuse him (as some have) for being a 'whingeing Pom' who
could not stand up to Aussie reality. We should only admire
Lawrence for throwing so much psychological light upon
the spiritual problems confronting Australian society. No
writer, English or Australian, before him had made the
inside life of the Australian psyche so clear and transparent;
no-one had expressed the psychic difficulties and
complexities with such human immediacy and with such
poignant urgency. At the end of *Kangaroo*, Somers-
Lawrence wistfully hears the 'call' of Australia and wonders
when it will be answered:

> From far off, from down long fern-dark avenues there
> seemed to be the voice of Australia, calling low ...
> [He] knew [it] would go on calling for long ages before
> it got any adequate response, in human beings.
> (p. 399)

5

The demonic interior
A cautionary tale

I would now like to turn to Patrick White's classic novel *Voss* (1957) to illustrate the serious problems that are discovered in the Australian psyche. Voss and his party of explorers set out from Sydney to 'conquer' the outback and to 'win' it for white colonial authority. Despite the external heroics of this great expedition, we discover that the real motivational force behind Voss and his explorers is the desire for death and disintegration. On the surface, life is lived according to the heroic patriarchal pattern, but underneath a fierce sacrificial impulse holds sway, an impulse that is not transformative because it operates completely unconsciously. If Voss knows what he is doing then his self-sacrifice may be redemptive, and it may be an act that positively links Australian society with the elemental earth. But unconscious acts of sacrifice do not heal wounds or close gaps; they are profane and unsanctified offerings, which do not appease the archetypal source but merely arouse the expectation of further sacrifice. Involuntary sacrifice, as fairytales and myths make clear,[1] turns the unconscious into an insatiable monster, which will continue to make more and greater demands until its needs are consciously recognised.

If my own reading is correct, the notion that Voss is a destructive psychotic rather than a great explorer of new lands calls into question the proudly heroic and nationalistic status that is accorded Voss by both Patrick White and the Australian public.[2] Voss is constructed by White's authorial commentary as a worthy, if somewhat arrogant, adventurer who sees the light at the end and is finally reconciled to his Maker upon his death. In this same way, Voss is celebrated in the literary and operatic world (notably in David Malouf's opera *Voss*), and in our secondary schools and universities, as a national legend or heroic figure who symbolises the progressive spirit in Australian society. In the 1965 secondary school edition of *Voss*, the academic editor tells his young readers that Voss is 'a hero [who] marches confidently into the future'; he 'leads his composite band into the interior not for the sake of material rewards but to help create a national legend'.[3]

To my mind this is a comforting, if also distorting, fiction which may accord with national goals and ego-ambitions, but which is far from the truth of the story. Beneath the imposed intellectual framework of this novel there is a much darker tale to read of deliberate self-destruction and antiheroic disintegration. This darker story accords with what we have already seen in relation to the nihilistic and downward impulse in the Australian psyche: the desire to abandon the inauthentic colonial self and become one with the land in a sacrificial death. This aspect of the Australian psyche tragically remains unconscious in our society, and thus the refusal to read Voss's story in this context is broadly symptomatic of our serious national blindness. The presence of a self-destructive dynamism in our national character does not fit in with our sense of being 'young and free', nor with our healthy, positive, and practical self-image. Our greatest Australian novel is a tale of ritual suicide, but the nation hardly wants to recognise this, and so instead we construct Voss as an achieving hero.

Seeing through to the archetypal structure

Some literary critics take the view that reading novels for what lies beyond or outside the author's intentions shows bad faith on the part of the critic. They argue that such readings demonstrate an unduly suspicious attitude toward art, and that readers should feel obliged to read the text as the author intended it to be read. However, this view disregards the revolutionary contributions made by psychoanalysis to literary study this century. Postmodern literary theory is richly informed by Freudian and Lacanian views of creativity, which are intensely alert to the autonomous nature of creative work, to the possibility of gaps and ruptures of meaning, and are never shocked when text and author fail to match or agree. This conflict is fundamental to the psychoanalytic insight that creativity wells up from the unconscious psyche and may very often— perhaps even mostly—diverge from what the conscious mind of the author 'thinks' or intends. Here is where a Jungian reading of literature converges strongly with contemporary literary theory. The traditional humanist 'celebration' of the artist as all-knowing intuitive source is apparently affronted and disturbed by such thinking. Until the unconscious can be valued as an independent and semi-autonomous fount of literary creativity, we will continue to be plagued by sentimental idealisations of the artist, and naively assume that the author's conscious position is identical with the text itself.

> It would be better that I should go barefoot, and alone. I know. But it is useless to try to convey to others the extent of that knowledge.[4]

The archetypal imagery of the novel relates to Voss's erotic journey toward the womb of the earth mother. Voss is entranced by the death-dealing mother, and throughout the story it is the apparition of Laura Trevelyan—an interior figure based upon Voss's brief meeting with the real Laura in Sydney—who acts as the dark inspiratrice who lures the German toward his ritual suicide. Laura is what Jung would call the Ghostly Lover, or demonic anima;[5] an archetypal figure who seduces the ego away from life and offers the prospect of an ecstatic state of unity in death. Voss is completely overwhelmed by this image of a blissful 'marriage' with the demon-lover, and he can therefore be counted as one of Barcroft Boake's 'dead men' who keep 'endless tryst' with the sacrifice-demanding earth.[6]

In stark contrast to this bleak archetypal structure is the redemptive Christian pattern that Patrick White super-imposes upon the narrative. In numerous commentaries and in rhetorical moments in the text, White announces that Voss is a tragic hero who is about to be 'humbled' by the Father God. These claims are not borne out by the novel, and actually appear to repress or stifle the grim reality of the human sacrifice to the bloodthirsty earth. I should point out that I have no personal quarrel with Christianity as such, but I have a high regard for getting the archetypal context of a situation right. If a story, vision, or dream-sequence points to a specific mytheme, it does so for good reason, and any attempt to obscure or transfer the archetypal context can be seen only as an unconscious defence mechanism designed to hide certain unsalient aspects of the myth.

The Australian earth is portrayed in this novel as a vicious and violent destroyer. I believe that the demonic quality of Patrick White's continental interior is especially intense because the need to sacrifice is so strongly repressed. As Jung made clear,[7] there is a kind of compensatory relationship between the attitude of the ego and the stance of the archetypal field: to some extent the unconscious reflects back the face that is turned toward it. If the ego clings obsessively to the 'edge' and denies the centre, or the inner depths of being, then the unconscious will be perceived as a terrible antagonist that strives to destroy human life. If there were some attempt at dialogue or interaction between the ego and the need for sacrifice, the demonic quality of what transpires would in all probability be reduced. The world of this novel is rigidly divided into Voss's party, who freely abandon themselves to destruction, and the so-called 'huddlers' in the fortified cities, who would never venture into the interior for fear of disintegration. (This opposition will be explored presently.) So long as there is no middle ground between unconscious indulgence and conscious denial, Australian society can never come of age nor integrate the cultural and religious meaning of its own compulsion toward sacrifice.

The cult of the dead

Voss is the passive instrument of an archetypal power:

> There he was, striped by moonlight and darkness, the stale air moving round him, very softly. Voss himself did not move. Rather was he moved by a dream, Palfreyman sensed. Through some trick of moonlight or uncertainty of behaviour, the head became detached for a second and appeared to have been fixed upon a beam of the wooden wall ...
>
> The moonlight returned Voss to the room. As he was moved back, his bones were creaking, and his skin had erupted in a greenish verdigis ...
>
> Next morning [Palfreyman] remarked:
>
> 'Mr Voss, do you know you were sleep-walking last night?' ...
>
> 'I have never been known to, before. Never,' he replied, but most irritably, as if refusing a crime with which he had been unjustly charged. (p. 177)

This is a fascinating sequence that points to the image of

Voss as an unknowing sleepwalker. His actions appear to be involuntary—'Voss himself did not move. Rather was he moved by a dream'. It is not Voss's will that is in control, but an unconscious mechanism that drives him from within. Naturally, Voss refuses to acknowledge this. He dismisses Palfreyman's remark as an 'unjust charge'. The reference to moonlight is important here: Voss's sleepwalking takes place 'under the indicator of that magnetic moon' (p. 176). He is held under a Luna spell, bewitched by the Goddess. Palfreyman imagines that Voss's head has been removed from his body as he walks out into the night. In a sense, this is a prefiguration of his decapitation at the hands of the Aboriginals in the desert. But in psychological terms Voss has already 'lost his head', he has lost his reason to the destructive forces of the psyche.

In relation to the other explorers, Voss acts as a hypnotised hypnotist who draws other men into the nightmare in which he is ensnared. His colleagues must already have a destructive impulse in them to be caught up in Voss's myth, but the leader acts as a satanic figure who brings to life their buried desires for self-annihilation. One follower is Frank Le Mesurier, who is also wedded to the idea of ecstatic release in death. Voss enjoins Le Mesurier to follow him on a mission of torture and self-mutilation:

> 'in this disturbing country, so far as I have become acquainted with it already, it is possible more easily to discard the inessential and to attempt the infinite. You will be burnt up most likely, you will have the flesh torn from your bones, you will be tortured probably in many horrible and primitive ways, but you will realize that genius of which you sometimes suspect you are possessed, and of which you will not tell me you are afraid.'
>
> Tempted, the young man was ... afraid—but ... he was also flattered.

> 'All right then,' said Le Mesurier ... 'What have I
> got to lose?'
> He was already thrilled by the immensity of
> darkness, and resented the approach of those lights
> which would reveal human substance, his own in
> particular. (pp. 35–6)

It is strange how this passage of the novel is frequently cited
in literary commentary with a complete absence of
awareness of its sado-masochistic component. Critics read
the phrase about 'attempting the infinite' and think of epic
journeys of spiritual and heroic discovery. But careful
attention has to be paid to the language and imagery. Voss
is inviting Le Mesurier to have the flesh torn from his
bones, to experience primitive torture, and to be destroyed
in the desert. This is not merely metaphorical colouring:
Voss actually means it. One naturally thinks of the
demonic cult leaders of this century who have lured
followers to a painful death by the temptation of greatness
and spiritual reward. In this way, Voss seduces not only Le
Mesurier but also many readers into believing that his
mission is genuinely redemptive. Le Mesurier is 'tempted'
and also 'flattered' by Voss's recognition of his potential
greatness. The trap has been set, and both readers and
characters fall into it.

Harry Robarts is a young recruit who is also compelled
into servitude by Voss's powerful death-romanticism.
Robarts is helpless before the German's tyrannical and
fascistic power. Turner is a drunkard and a 'derelict soul'
(p. 42), whose longing for annihilation has expressed itself
in his alcoholism. For Turner the expedition holds no
spiritual pretensions whatsoever, but is merely a chance to
self-destruct in grand style, rather than dissolve
anonymously in the gutters of Sydney. It is Turner who
readily admits the perverse side of the expedition and who
declares that he has 'Contracted with a practisin' madman

... for a journey to hell an' back' (p. 43). To hell to be sure, but 'back' again is wishful thinking.

A follower of a different order is the English natural scientist Palfreyman. Palfreyman's motivation for joining the party is to 'atone' for what he perceives as his wrongdoings toward his sister, wrongdoings partly inspired by his overwhelming incestuous desires. What better way to enact his atonement than by offering himself as a human sacrifice to an archaic maternal landscape? Palfreyman and Voss both experience the Australian landscape in mythologised form, as a feminine figure or womb-matrix. At several points in the story Palfreyman's sister appears as an apparition in the desert, and as his death approaches she takes him by the hand and leads him into the beyond. For Palfreyman, Voss is a kind of deliverer, a leader who enables him to live out his incestuous and suicidal fantasies in symbolic form, as an erstwhile explorer of foreign lands.

The woman who unmakes men

Voss shows us how the disturbed relationship between conscious and unconscious in the Australian psyche impacts negatively on the relationship between the sexes. Since the unconscious spontaneously represents itself as feminine, and since the Australian unconscious is desperate for organic connection with consciousness, men continually experience women as overwhelming figures who appear to want to devour and consume them. Women thus inspire fear and dread in men, resulting in widespread misogyny in Australian society, and in a significant homosexual flight from woman.[8] We pay very dearly, in our sexuality and in our standard of human society, for our collective disregard for the unconscious.

But because there is a deep archetypal compulsion toward fusion with the maternal unconscious, White's men alternately flee from and bury themselves in the 'devouring' embrace of the feminine. In White's writing, the desire for sexual oblivion in the feminine is always enacted symbolically and abstractly, in the encounter with landscape. Nowhere in the dozen or more major novels do we find positive accounts of male–female sexual relations, but we frequently discover male characters involved in ecstatic quasi-sexual relations with nature. It is important to observe that Voss's ecstatic 'relationship' with Laura Trevelyan takes place only when there are huge distances of desert country between them. We could justly say that distance is not an obstacle to their love, but an essential precondition for it. If, somehow, the lovers were to be physically reunited, the romance would dissolve immediately. This is because the actual female body for White carries the brute image of the devouring matrix. White constructs an infantile Australian society where mature sexual relationships are not yet possible: men find emotional security in other male company, and sexual release can be found only in engagement with the nonhuman elemental world.

As Voss's party is set to embark, Palfreyman and Laura exchange polite farewells, when Palfreyman is suddenly overcome by a feeling of drowning and dissolution:

> Laura looked toward Palfreyman. As he withdrew through the already considerable crowd, he received the impression of a drowning that he was unable to avert, in a dream through which he was sucked inevitably back.
>
> Ah, Laura was crying out, bending down through the same dream, extending her hand in its black glove; you are my only friend, and I cannot reach you.
> (p. 109)

This is the first real indication that Laura is to act as a Siren-figure in the novel, a figure who entices men to their ruin. Palfreyman feels he is being drawn into a disorienting vortex, that he is being 'sucked inevitably back'. As the ego enters the unconscious, it loses its orientation and stability, and the unconscious, represented by Laura, appears to take command. 'You are my only friend, and I cannot reach you': this expresses the deep longing of the unconscious for contact with consciousness. Such contact is always ambivalent for the nascent ego: it feels pleasure and pain in being dissolved in a greater psychic field.

As the expedition moves toward the continental interior it is the pleasurable side of egoic dissolution that predominates at the beginning. Voss feels he is entering a 'gentle, healing landscape' (p. 124): 'At once the hills were enfolding him … and he was touching [them] and was not surprised at their suave flesh' (p. 139). Soon the complete mythologisation of Laura Trevelyan is under way, and she becomes identical with the maternal earth: 'He continued to think about the young woman, there on the banks of the river, where the points of her wooden elbows glimmered in the dusk' (p. 152).

> All the immediate world was soon swimming in the same liquid green. She was clothed in it. Green shadows almost disguised her face, where she walked amongst the men, to whom, it appeared, she was known, as others were always known to one another, from childhood, or by instinct. (p. 198)

Laura emerges as the Eternal Feminine, clothed in the green of the landscape, a woman known to all men 'from childhood', for she is now a completely archetypal figure, and hence transpersonal: a shared experience. Voss is personally affronted by Laura's apparent familiarity with other men, and by her only casual interest in himself: 'he was the passing acquaintance, at whom she did glance once, since it was unavoidable'. The ambivalent character of the archetypal feminine begins to reveal itself. The individual ego is not unique or special to an archetypal being: it is finite, temporal, and almost incidental compared with the eternality of the collective archetype. Voss is already beginning to feel diminished and inconsequential before his mystic bride. Laura's ambivalent aspect is further indicated: 'Then he noticed how her greenish flesh was spotted with blood'. The dramatic shift from the splendorous woman clothed in green to the image of 'greenish flesh spotted with blood' indicates the full paradoxical reality and archetypal range of this mythic figure. The archetypal feminine contains splendour and terror, and her nature is as equally reflected in the blood-thirsty Goddess Kali as in the amorous Aphrodite or Venus.

Voss dreams that he enters a pond of lilies with his beloved, only to find that he is sucked toward death. 'Now they were swimming so close they were joined at the waist, and were the same flesh of lilies, their mouths, together, were drowning in the same love-stream' (p. 187). This is a classic representation of the demonic and otherworldly anima, as of the Germanic death-romanticism that underlies this novel. Voss is drawn ineluctably toward the seductive maw, which seems only too eager to make a meal of him. Holding the womb-shaped death-lily in her hands, Laura informs Voss that she has the power to control him, since it is 'the woman who unmakes men, to make saints' (p. 188). The dream correctly reverses the attitude of his conscious mind, showing him in a helpless position, at the mercy of the castrating maw. The dream also points to the consolation prize that is offered the earth's loved son: an illusion of sainthood. The disintegration of the mind is an event that pleases the earth and satiates her hunger, and in myth and fairytale the Earth Goddess frequently tricks her victims into believing that death at her hands is a death rich in spiritual reward.

The hypnotised cavalcade is plagued by drought, heat, treacherous ground, crawling insects, famine and disease. Voss's horse is attacked by a snake, and the rider's head is gashed by a tree. In the presence of these painful events, Voss notices that his otherworldly bride is radiant and smiling:

> When they had remounted and were riding on, Voss wondered how much of himself he had given into her hands. For he had become aware that the mouth of the young woman was smiling. It was unusually full and compassionate. Approbation must have gone to his head, for he continued unashamedly to contemplate her pleasure, and to extract from it pleasure of his own. They were basking in the same radiance, which had begun to emanate from the hitherto lustreless earth. (pp. 208–9)

The destructive impact of a brute landscape gives way to the ghostly smile of his demonic inspiratrice. It gives her great satisfaction to see him ruining his body and spirit in pursuit of her eternal embrace. Because the earth-woman delights in his ritual disintegration, the loved son is able to glean 'pleasure of his own', for his greatest fulfilment is to serve she who must be obeyed. Sado-masochistic pleasure is a characteristic feature of an ego that is possessed by an archetypal content: the destruction of the self is painful, but the experience of becoming absorbed into a greater archetypal figure yields strange pleasure.[9]

Palfreyman's fate reveals most dramatically the sordid horror of this archetypal entrancement. On the eve of his death he falls into a state of delirium, and his mythic inspiratrice appears to lure him away: 'One side of him Voss, the other his lady sister, in her cloak that was the colour of ashes. Towards morning her hand took his hand and they walked into the distant embers, which hurt horribly, but which he must continue to endure, as he was unfitted for anything else' (p. 282). The fantasy voyage with the eternal feminine 'hurt horribly' because this is nothing less than a journey into disintegration. But the knowledge that this represents the fulfilment of his personal destiny provides some comfort and assurance. In his final moments, he walks unarmed toward a group of hostile desert tribesmen. He declares that he will 'trust to his faith' (p. 341), and even the equally possessed Voss has to admit that his claim 'sounded terribly weak'. Palfreyman becomes 'more transparent' with each step and in a climactic moment he feels ecstatically united with his sister. When the spear strikes his chest, he bursts into a fit of laughter. This is the demonic laughter of a loved son who has finally returned to the matrix. The mythic pattern and process of the novel is suddenly made appallingly clear.

The contrary impulse: desert mutilation versus city barricades

In complete contrast to these scenes of frenzied self-mutilation are the scenes of the fear-ridden 'huddlers' back home. Significantly, during the course of the epic expedition, alternate chapters of the novel keep returning us to the safe, enclosed world of Mr Edmund Bonner and his bourgeois circle in Sydney. This group has a completely negative attitude toward the unconscious: they skate around on the surface of life, clinging to what is comfortable and rational, forever preoccupied with the petty and trivial tasks of keeping up appearances. The juxtaposing of these contrary worlds in the novel has more than a structural significance. Here we find the opposite side of the Australian psyche at work, the side which, as I have suggested, most likely *forces* the archetypal interior into a demonic stance by way of necessary compensation. Because the Australian social awareness is—or has been—

so petty and trite, so heavily fortified against the elemental psyche, the unconscious has had to exert its forceful and even destructive attraction upon us. To put it more succinctly: the unconscious interior 'devours' because the conscious exterior defends.

This strangely systemic relationship between a defended conscious and a demonic unconscious is borne out by the fact that it is Mr Edmund Bonner who financially sponsors and underwrites Voss's desert expedition. Although Bonner would never himself venture into the continental interior or into his own unconscious, he is happy to provide backing and support for Voss's adventure: a defended consciousness invites and even encourages demonic self-mutilation in the unconscious. These two elements are co-dependent. This is true also for the archetypal construction of gender in Australia: it is only because the masculine is so defended, closed, unresponsive, that the feminine is forced to become (or appear) insistent, strident, overbearing.

A certain kind of twinning of Voss and Bonner takes place in the novel; everything Bonner asserts Voss denies, and vice versa.

'A pity that you huddle,' said the German. 'Your country is of great subtlety' (p. 11). This is matched by Bonner's negative attitude toward the interior:

> 'I am inclined to believe, Mr Voss, that you will
> discover a few black-fellers, and a few flies, and
> something resembling the bottom of the sea.
> That is my humble opinion.' (p. 62)

Sometimes Voss and Bonner are too obviously, too simply opposed:

> They were two blue-eyed men, of a different blue.
> Voss would frequently be lost to sight in his, as birds
> are in sky. But Mr Bonner would never stray far

beyond familiar objects. His feet were on the earth.
(p. 17)

'You are quite certain you are ready to undertake
such a great expedition?' he now dared to ask.
'Naturally,' the German replied.
He had his vocation, it was obvious, and equally
obvious that his patron would not understand.
(p. 20)

As the men study the map of the inland 'Mr Bonner read the words, but Voss saw the rivers. He followed them in their fretful course. He flowed, festering with green scum'. Voss concentrates on his mystic dissolution, but Bonner sees only surface reality and the ego's standpoint. The relationship is altogether too algebraic, and we sometimes suspect that they are split off, one-dimensional aspects of a larger psychic potential. If White's interior and exterior impulses engaged in meaningful dialogue, we might enter a fuller, more human imaginal world. Voss could be held back from his desperate ritual suicide by Bonner's caution, and Bonner stirred from his sloth and indolence by Voss's drive.

The complexity of *Voss* suffers from this schizoid splitting. The to and fro movement between opposite societies becomes tedious, the two worlds of the novel seem irreconcilable. The contrasts become more pronounced and disturbing as the story quickens toward its climax. As Voss and his party become increasingly manic in their search for mystic dissolution, Bonner and his associates become, if it is possible, more fanatically rigid and defensive in their empty persona-lives. The point is that, no matter how much White despises the Sydney huddlers and the neurotically barricaded, he is psychologically bound to represent them in an increasingly defensive way, because the human instinct for survival and ego-stability must keep pace with the psychotic drive toward disintegration. These are twin aspects of the one psychic structure, and thank God for it, because otherwise the unchecked desire toward ecstatic dissolution could have wiped us all out long before this.

Within the inland group the survival instinct makes a partial appearance. After witnessing the horrifying spectacle of Palfreyman's ritual death and Le Mesurier's increasing madness, it becomes apparent to some of the more sober members that they are involved in a cult of the dead. It is Turner who strives to create a split-off group, and he urges Judd and Angus to support him in a bid for return to safety and refuge. Turner announces that Voss and his inner circle are intent on 'mad things' and strive to 'blow up the world'. 'People of that kind will destroy what you and I know' says the newly-converted 'huddler' in the desert landscape. Finally, Judd is forced to recognise the cult-like nature of the expedition, and decides to lead a band of rebels from 'the deserts of mysticism' to 'his own fat paddocks' (p. 345).

The mutinous party does not survive. Turner and Angus die agonising deaths on their attempted return, and Judd survives only in the flesh, for his mind is tortured and insane by the time he reaches civilisation. Even as he arrives at his former property, Judd finds that his wife and children have died and that his fat paddocks are ruined. This is to be expected in White's fictional world, for once the personality has set foot in the deep interior it tends to be shattered by the experience. The rebels disintegrate like the others, only their deaths are without ecstasy because they have turned their backs on the prospect of quasi-sexual union with the eternal feminine.

Last rites: keeping endless tryst

After this disruption, 'the division led by Voss seemed to move with greater ease' (p. 358). This is to be expected because the unconscious resistance to the expedition has been removed or exorcised by the mutinous party. Now the renegade element can run toward an ecstatic death without any moral interference. Voss's party reaches a circular plain of stones, which is the mythic locus, the goal of the journey. As they approach the sacred site, the desert Aboriginals line up on either side of them, as if to provide an escort for their mythic homecoming. But as they move toward the centre of the quartz field the Aboriginals close in behind them, and at once they feel imprisoned. They are now inside the stony womb of the earth mother, which is pleased to welcome them inside and to celebrate their entry, and even more pleased to capture them forever. The eternal feminine without mercy hath thee in thrall.

Le Mesurier senses immediately that his destiny has been fufilled: he stumbles toward a dead tree and cuts his throat with a pocket-knife. This is a classic image of the self-mutilating son of the Goddess. Attis castrated himself beneath a tree and bled to death. He destroyed his manhood in a state of frenzy, crying 'For thee, Cybele!' as he flung his severed phallus to the ground.[10] Attis's blood was supposed to rejuvenate the earth, to please the Goddess and to cause her to bring on the spring and 'make the world green'.[11] In his Rimbaud-like prose-poem, Le Mesurier writes: 'Flesh is for hacking … My blood will water the earth and make it green' (p. 297). In like manner, the blood that pours from Voss's decapitated head is imaged as an earth-offering: 'His blood ran out upon the dry earth, which drank it up immediately' (p. 394). Le Mesurier ends his savage poem with an incantatory hymn to the spirit of the earth, expressing his desire to be as one with the elements, to be 'everywhere and nowhere' at the same time. A mythic process has taken control, he identifies with the pagan sacrificial son, and his self-mutilation beneath the tree carries out to the letter the archaic celebration of the Earth Goddess.

As Voss enters the final stage of his self-torture, his mystic bride stands in the wings, whispering all kinds of encouragement and assurances. '"Do you see now?" she asked. "Man is God decapitated. That is why you are bleeding"' (p. 364). This over-blown rhetoric about Voss's apparent 'achievement' of transcendence can be found throughout the last sections of the novel, distorting Voss's (and the reader's) understanding of what is taking place. Depth psychology has found that this is one of the secondary characteristics of archetypal possession: an archetype that has taken full possession of the personality has an inflating effect upon the ego: it 'puffs up' the personality by whispering all manner of lies and grand delusions.[12] In this way, too, Voss's dismemberment and disintegration is misrepresented as an achievement of humility: 'Now that he is humble,' Laura announces, '[and] has learnt that he is not God ... he is nearest to becoming so' (p. 387). The incredible thing about these delusions of grandeur is that so many readers and critics swallow them whole. It is clear that Voss is an unknowing victim of a demonic complex, and yet most conventional accounts of this text represent Voss as an heroic achiever who finally attains Christ-like humility and divine status. The real problem is that we in secular society do not understand the language of myths or archetypes, we have no way of knowing who or what drives human personality, and so we cannot distinguish sainthood from ritual suicide, or a demonic complex from divine inspiration.

As Voss dies he has a final vision of Laura as the Medusa-headed Gorgon (pp. 383, 386), a demonic archetypal figure with ancient associations with death, madness, and dismemberment. And as if that is not enough, as his head is hacked off by order of the native women, he dreams at the end that Laura is an old, archaic Aboriginal woman who hands him the death-lily that has haunted his dreams since his early youth. Image upon image arises of the devouring Earth Goddess and her grotesque cult of the dead, but there is still Laura's rhetoric about Christian sainthood and spiritual transcendence. Never was a textual framework of interpretation more artificial or inflating.

The interior life of this country, from which our spiritual and archetypal problems arise, is governed by matriarchal forces and chthonic-feminine contents that require their own frame of reference and mythopoetic understanding. The argument of the above four chapters is that if we paid specific care and attention to our relationship with nature, to the maternal earth and the archetypal feminine, we would be in much better shape culturally and spiritually than we are today. If we gave more to the feminine in its many aspects and expressions, 'she' would not have to take so much from us. If we gave consciously to the Earth Mother, we would not, like Voss and his party, be violently subdued by her.

Re-enchantment

6

Relaxing barriers, admitting the other

> The numinous presents itself as something 'wholly other' (*ganz andere*), something basically and totally different.
>
> — MIRCEA ELIADE[1]

Beyond the demonic or romantic other

In *Intruders in the Bush*, John Carroll correctly observes that 'there are two extremes, either the illusion of a cosy and mysteriously redemptive Bush exorcised of threat, or the intimidating vision of an unthinkable desert land that is pure horror'.[2] As we have seen, Australians construct images of the land that are either paradisal or demonic. We have traditions of art and literature at both ends of this mythopoetic spectrum. For the bush as heaven (or Arcadia, a lesser kind of heaven), we have 'Banjo' Paterson, Henry Kingsley, Katherine Prichard, and the Heidelberg School of painters. For the bush as hell we have Henry Lawson, Marcus Clarke, D.H. Lawrence, Patrick White, and the paintings, for instance, of Albert Tucker and Sidney Nolan. It is inevitable that these mythological images are projected upon the Australian landscape, since myths always determine and shape our experience of environment, especially our experience of the significant sacred other. And in Australia, 'God is a vast blue and pale-gold and red-brown landscape'.[3]

My own view is that if either extreme gains the

ascendancy cultural evolution and spiritual development cannot take place. Australian culture can only remain stagnant. If we see the psychological interior as Arcadia, we are projecting an ego-syntonic ideal and are engaging in a Freudian wish-fulfilment, that, as Carroll says, is a 'cosy illusion', leading to complacency, inertia, stasis on the part of the ego and the culture. When Arcadia is projected, the other is 'exorcised of threat' and is not sufficiently *other* to shock the ego into any new recognitions or new levels of consciousness. From this arises what Ronald Conway calls the 'great Australian stupor'. I grew up with a deep resistance and even a mild sense of nausea with regard to the bush poems of A.B. Paterson, which placed humanity in a comfortable, bourgeois leather saddle, riding dreamily through friendly countryside. This did not tally with my own experience of landscape, and seemed altogether too smug, colonialist, heroic, and self-satisfied. It is a form of denial, a systematic attempt to rob the other of its transformative power.

On the other hand, if the bush is 'pure horror', there can be no development either. When the interior is demonic and ego-dystonic, the ego will not venture into it, and thus cannot be transformed. The ego is frozen in terror, and condemns itself to a petty existence at the surface of life— as Voss says to his Sydney patrons, 'it is a pity that you huddle'. Below the paranoid surface, however, dark and anarchistic impulses move in the opposite direction (the huddlers actually sponsor Voss's ritual suicide). The ego is no match for the archetypal other, and when the other is denied it makes itself felt in destructive and negative ways. In spite of the ego's resistance, the other draws energy and human life toward itself, as if in a trance or dream (Voss is in a trance state, as are the girls at Hanging Rock). What the demonic and Arcadian scenarios have in common is an inability to make true concessions or willing sacrifices to the other. Ego and other, conscious and unconscious, humanity and God, do not relate to each other in creative, redemptive, or mutually transforming ways, but operate on different levels, engaging in occasional, and fatal, collision courses.

The Australian ego must learn to recognise that the other—whether the landscape, the divine being, or the deep unconscious—is infinitely greater than itself, is not simply good or evil and cannot be caught in stereotypes of heaven or hell. The other is complex, awesome, subtle, many-sided, and must be entered into relationship with. All that is required at the outset, in order to break the typical Australian cycles of stupor, inertia, and destructivity, is a healthy respect for the other. With that new respect, focus, or attention, the necessary sacrifice of part of the ego's domain has begun and genuine transformation can occur. All-powerful gods, goddesses, archetypes, or complexes cannot make this happen; it has to happen from the human side, and that is why this relationship is called 'sacrifice', because the ego is made to feel that it is giving up part of its own life in order to gain a greater life through the sacred. As we negotiate this sacrifice, the demonic face of the Australian interior will disappear, because we will be giving consciously and willingly of ourselves; the mythic interior will not be forced to devour us. When the ego changes, so does the unconscious, since these two forms of psychic reality are deeply and organically linked.

Postmodern landscape: the self as other

> Je est un autre.
> I is an other.
> — RIMBAUD[4]

I believe that what we see in contemporary art, literature, music, and in some progressive social attitudes is *an increased sense of openness to the other*. Contemporary Australian writing can virtually be summed up as a literature of the other. 'Other', 'abnormal', 'aberrant' types of people are explored, revealing new resonances, depths, and insecurities about 'normal' people. Everything taken for granted is unpacked, disassembled, and re-explored. Contemporary fictions are about Asians in Australia and Australians in Asia. There is a significant body of writing by and about Aboriginal Australians, and there are stories about people who are both Aboriginal and Euro-Australian. The once-simple topic of national and personal identity has been exploded, everything is complex and complicated, refracted, distorted.[5] Otherness has hit us with enormous cultural force; we are awash in the sea of otherness, and that is the best definition I know for the 'postmodern condition'.

In the postmodern writing of Jolley, Murnane, Malouf, Garner, Winton, Carey, and others, *even the self is an other*. The self is opened, unravelled, and its hidden desires and impulses explored. Elizabeth Jolley deconstructs the self, and finds alarming incongruities, absurdities, and contradictions at the heart of the most ordinary Australian 'self'.[6] Helen Garner wanders through the complex world of the *inner* suburbs, finding incredible pain, anguish and hurt in the apparently bland surfaces, and showing unexpected sources of revelation, mystery, and transcendence.[7] Tim Winton shows that human chaos and disorder can be the very opening through which the Otherworld enters human reality and transforms it from within.[8] Gerald Murnane virtually dissolves literal reality into metaphor, more interested in the hidden possibilities lurking in every moment than in the reporting of what actually happens.[9] The unconscious has erupted from the depths, and makes unprecedented claims on reality, so that the fantastic and the real are now difficult to separate. The old comforting fiction we once called 'the Bush' has disintegrated, leaving mystery, uncertainty, doubt in its wake. It is not simply, as I have heard said, that landscape is no longer a theme that interests writers, but rather that what we once called 'landscape' has gone through a complete transformation, so that it is almost no longer recognisable. At the hands of Gerald Murnane, landscape has become internalised, metaphysical, a kind of 'spiritual geography'[10] where boundaries are fluid and changing. Neither the self nor the landscape is a solid, defined object, as it once was. We have stepped out of the old Newtonian 'building-block' image of reality and entered instead a world closer to the new physics and quantum science, where 'things' have been dissolved into energies, and even energies are not mechanical, predictable, objective, but changing, mystical, and affected by the subject who observes them.

The postmodern condition is not a mere invention of the university or of artists. It is an important cultural shift in which the once-solid world has been dissolved in the ambiguity of otherness. I am not sure how 'post'-modern this is, because expressionist and abstract artists a hundred years ago were dissolving solidity and form, creating new perceptions of the world and new syntheses of fact and fiction. James Joyce was doing exactly this, in narrative fiction, eighty years ago. But what has been brewing in the arts for some time has now expressed itself as a worldwide 'condition', and it is exciting to find that science has not resisted this trend but has gone with it and has actually arrived, simultaneously as it were, at the same new premises and findings. Although I dislike reading Derrida, I do agree with him that the new condition should not be cause for complaint or fear, but that we should attempt to discover, perhaps perversely, the 'joy' within this confusion and ontological chaos.

Whether it likes it or not, Australia is deeply affected by the postmodern moment, and the fluidity of boundaries that comes with this moment is well timed to coincide with the necessary destructuring of the heavily defended and fortified Australian consciousness. The national psyche is already involved in significant change and is substantially different to what it was even twenty-five years ago. Some will think this is obvious and no big deal, but those who understand archetypal processes and patterns will appreciate that change normally does not take place rapidly at the deeper levels of the psyche. The surface of life can be riddled with shifts and changes, while underneath the archetypes can be unmoved by what takes place above. However, we are going through a genuine psychological reorientation, where surface and depth are changing simultaneously in Australian culture. It is a crucial moment (the *kairos* or 'right moment'), when new foundations for the future can be set in place, and old stereotypes and patterns be laid to rest.

Admitting social and political otherness

In Australian social and political life, significant readjustments to various expressions of the other have been occurring for some time. However, we still have to be very cautious about these apparent changes in sociopolitical life. Are Australians gaining real respect for the other, or are we simply being bombarded by otherness, so that we can no longer avoid it? *Otherness* threatens the old structures at every level of postmodern experience. We have been forced into new awareness (however limited) about Aboriginal people, women, gays, ecology and the environment, other cultures, other races, Asia (possibly the most potent symbol of the other at the moment). We are forced to notice religions and myths other than our own 'myth' of secular materialism, political ideas other than the ones we have long held, football codes we have long ignored, sexual preferences and habits other than our own. The new status accorded to the newly arrived migrant is an indicator of cultural change. In the past, the migrant was frowned upon and prejudiced against by an over-defended national ego, whereas today the migrant is highly regarded and in some quarters even idealised as a personification of the otherness that Australia has come to embrace.

Australia has finally given up the myth that it is a homogenous, unified Anglo-Saxon monoculture, a myth that was fiercely promoted during the major decades of Australian nationalism. Instead, a new myth has arisen which portrays Australia as a diverse, pluralistic, multicultural society, in which Aboriginal people have a special place as the original inhabitants of this land. Whereas before it was bad to be different and good to conform to prevailing stereotypes, now certain kinds of (often stylised) difference are celebrated and championed by both the government and the public alike. Some cynics argue that 'difference' is a fad which is paid lip-service only, but I feel it has at least one foot in the door. In political and economic terms, Australia has given up the fantasy of itself as ruggedly independent and materially self-sufficient ('riding on the sheep's back'). Politicians now tell us that Australia must participate more fully in the global and Asia-Pacific region, and that it must judge itself not by its own standards but by world economic indicators and by multinational standards. Australians have to 'wake up' from their long stupor, emerge from their protective cocoon, and face the real world of international economic and political forces. 'We have turned a closed, protected, defensive economy into an open one,' boasted Barry Jones, a key figure in the Australian Labor Party, during an election campaign in 1993. Such openness and inclusiveness, which many more traditional Anglo-Celtic Australians fail to understand or appreciate, is nevertheless the style of the future.

The old stoical, laconic 'masculinist' national persona is now widely viewed as anachronistic and burdensome. Stoicism, so revered in pioneer days, is today more likely to be seen as a code of repression and psychological armouring. Laconicism, once so highly valued, is now viewed as a social and personal handicap, a refusal to be expressive and articulate, a choking of the 'natural' desire for communication. A great many of the values and attitudes taken for granted today are straight from the United States, and heavily influenced by the religion of self-expression, which is integral to the hugely popular 'personal growth movement' from America. The old masculinism of 1950s Australia gets a huge hiding in the contemporary university, where it is read as patriarchal oppression. Also, the once-idealised white 'pioneers' and 'settlers' tend to be regarded today with some suspicion, as unlawful intruders, invaders of Aboriginal land. Our previous cultural habit of systematically denying the aboriginal and the indigenous is now denounced as cultural imperialism, neocolonialism, racism, and 'white supremacist ideology'.

The political and cultural side of our necessary decolonisation or dearmouring is what is studied and preached today in all humanities and social science schools in every tertiary institution in the country. The university-educated are now well versed in the art of collapsing, deconstructing, decolonising the rigid structures of the colonial past. But we still know precious little about the depth psychological and spiritual side of this cultural dearmouring. Nor are we alert to the dangers inherent in our own destructuring programme. It is assumed today that to break down, to unpack or unravel is to liberate and inspire new life, but there is little attention paid to the possible negative and destructive side of this process.

If we are hit with too much otherness, too much that is

'foreign' to the ego, reintegration and reorientation will not take place, and there will be widespread psychosocial disruption. This is the view that Geoffrey Blainey attempted to put some years ago, but he was attacked by a 'politically correct' media and academia. The other is politically correct at present, and anyone who dares speak out in defence of the old social ego, which has to cope with the other, is given short shrift. But in spite of the push toward increased openness and newness, we witness a generalised cultural backlash. Politically, the forces of conservatism are moving to reinforce the barriers that have been relaxed over recent years. The desire for certainty, closure, stability is felt today in many areas of social and political life. In the university, there is a tendency to want to seal over the wounds and ruptures brought by postmodern sensibility, a desire to strengthen traditional 'disciplines' and to get the world of knowledge back under control. In popular culture, we find nostalgia, or so-called 'Oztalgia', all around us, nostalgia for the 1940s, '50s, or '60s—for any decade except our own! Today we have radio stations that play only songs from the past. This social nostalgia and backward-looking gaze is to be expected in times of dramatic change, but the idealisation of the past is culturally dangerous if it prevents us from embracing the future.

Obviously a balance must be struck between openness and closure, change and stability, revolution and tradition. The social 'progressives' must realise that openness cannot be perpetual or permanent, and that the longing for stability cannot be underestimated since it is supported by the survival instinct and other instinctual and psychological mechanisms. We can only hope that fear of the new will not keep driving us back to a past that needs to be outgrown. In order to tolerate otherness, we need a certain respect for uncertainty, confusion, and difference. Australia requires a social ego, which respects and admits the other, yet which also recognises the claims of the past, of tradition, and of order.

In this atmosphere, the notion that Australia should become a republic gains momentum. In the past I have supported the republican movement, but I have come to feel ambivalent about it. The republic would appear to satisfy the progressive longing for change and the desire to break away from the old parental European culture. However, I suspect that at least some of the energy fuelling this debate arises from the desire to terminate uncertainty and anxiety by inventing a new cultural and personal order. The political idea of a republic may well be a good one, but if the idea is premature and inspired by a reactionary psychological need for closure and certainty, then the 'radical' gesture would be, ironically, to remain with the monarchical system and the postmodern condition.

The larger story: psychospiritual transformation

There are psychological and spiritual corollaries of these widely advertised and much discussed sociopolitical changes. We have already noted how contemporary Australian writers have been ringing in the changes: self as other, landscape as interiority, boundaries blurred between inner and outer, fantasy and reality, subject and object. In the world of art, the tidal wave of the other has already hit the old, sturdy, self-assured national character. Artists are almost by definition always ahead of their time; they are prophets of a psychological condition still to be realised in the wider community, which naturally strives valiantly to protect itself from change, to dull the impact of the new.

Australian society has done its best to ignore or repress the psychological changes that are imminent, or that have already been felt, preferring instead to monitor its self-transformation in purely political terms. The myth of politics (Greek *polis*, the state) is the most potent myth for this nation, and we love to exteriorise and project our psychic changes into the political process. Hence we feel more comfortable talking about our new receptivity to Asia, or our new 'open' economy, than about new openness to God, spirit, or the soul. And yet in this obsessive exteriorisation we lose so much, our spiritual story is lost, our inner transformation denied.

When the ego relaxes its barriers, or is assailed by the other, it is spontaneously transformed from within. There is a sudden upwelling from the unconscious as many psychic contents previously repressed are brought back to life, although these contents return in a new form. At first there is a sense of release from outworn and oppressive structures, a new feeling of joy as colonialist defences fall away. The mood of society, or at least that part of it that admits to these processes, shifts from one of limitation, constriction, closure, to one of relative fluidity and connectedness. We see this most notably in young Australians: a profound change of attitude with regard to identity, and the formation of an inclusive rather than exclusive sense of self. 'Self', at the present time, includes elements such as friends, neighbours, different cultures and races, which were all 'other' to me in the 1950s, yet are parts of 'self' to my daughter and her friends. Also, self has been extended to include aspects of environment and nature, so that an ecological sensibility is fundamental to the coming generation.

Fluidity in identity involves fluidity in gender and sexuality. Hence today, I sometimes have no idea at first whether some of my students are young men or women. This baffles and worries the oldies, but the young appear to thrive in this fluid world of gender. The most recent new event of national significance, the Sydney Gay Festival and Mardi Gras, is a massive symbol of this new experience of sexuality. Young people today sometimes flaunt their challenges to conventional sexuality, they forcefully display their fusions and confusions of dress, gender, genitalia, and style. This represents 'liberation' for some of the young, whereas for the old it is mostly read as chaos and disorder. My task here is not to sit in judgement on these social phenomena, but simply to provide a psychological context for them.

I have already indicated that the ego can be disoriented by too much sociopolitical otherness, and the same is true at the psychological level. As the old ego is eroded, there is always the dangerous possibility, most evident in the works of Patrick White, that a new stability or point of integration will not be achieved. Voss does not integrate the interior reality but is destroyed by it. Stan Parker in *The Tree of Man* cannot come to terms with what has been unleashed in his psyche, but is swamped by the unconscious. Only in *The Solid Mandala* is a new wholeness presented as a real possibility: the Jungian 'mandalas' arise in the novel as symbols of the new integration and cultural order that Australians must struggle to achieve in their postcolonial and postmodern society.[11] However, the ego-figure in that novel, Waldo Brown, cannot understand or accept his twin brother's transformative vision of the mandala, and the novel ends in chaos, death, and insanity. Arthur Brown's solid mandalas are reduced to mere playing marbles, boys' toys, and their healing symbolic potential is lost—to be recovered, I like to imagine, by future Australian artists.

Waldo Brown represents a brittle, narrow, constricted Australian ego, which is incapable of transformation. When this sort of ego contacts the unconscious, it is tragically annihilated. As Freud and Jung knew, a heavily armoured ego defends against the unconscious for good reason. If the ego has constructed itself as distant, detached, removed from emotional life, the unconscious can only be experienced as the 'enemy', which destructively overwhelms it. I believe that bits of our social ego will not be transformed but will simply be blown apart, especially the harder, metallic bits of our Ned Kelly mask that are incapable of undergoing change. The process of psychological reorientation will have its casualties: those who cling to the old outworn persona will be left behind by social change, and those who cannot handle the influx of new emotions will be overwhelmed by them. But there will be a core of psychological integrity in the Euro-Australian ego, which will meet the challenge that is put before it. The Australian national character is not all thin persona or masculine protest. There is spirit there as well, and even though that spirit may be young or frail, the time has come to allow it to mature and to expose it to the deep unconscious as never before.

Social embarrassment and spiritual hunger

'I've always thought that embarrassment is a key thing in the Australian consciousness. It's very profound.'

— HELEN GARNER

'In a moment of embarrassment there's a truth present ... The embarrassing moments are when control is imperfect, when other people see that there's some big force.'

— MICHAEL LEUNIG[12]

I believe we will experience a large amount of collective embarrassment and some guilt as Australians struggle to connect with contents and areas of the psyche that have previously been taboo or relegated to unconsciousness. This is because we have been taught for generations that interiority of any kind is a mere indulgence and that self-reflection is narcissism. Our cultural attitudes have been informed by progressive and positivist values that have helped serve the pioneer task of establishing European civilisation in Australia. Australians have been instructed, like children constantly harangued by an overzealous authority, to get on with the job, to cheer up, stop brooding; don't be morbid, don't be lazy. All our most frequently used social phrases and domestic clichés betray our terrible fear of the psychic depths.

Embarrassment will arise as we turn to face soul and spirit, which our positivist ethic has taught us to disparage and revile. Soul and spirit are felt to be superstitions of a bygone era, discredited by scientific advancement and rejected by secular society. It will hurt the pride of many Australians to have to admit to the existence of another reality—a reality long denied by 'enlightened' families, 'modern' institutions and 'progressive' groups. Yet when the unconscious is encountered as habitual defences fall away, soul and spirit turn out to be powerfully real, and the values that caused us to deny them will be revealed as empty prejudices supported by an inadequate ideology. But embarrassment, guilt, and shame will plague us before we can acknowledge the reality of spirit, because we will feel that we are letting the side down, not living up to modern expectations, and becoming somehow 'un-Australian'.

Because soul and spirit will be new territory for us, many Australians will be gullible, innocent, unable to discriminate between spirits, and so likely to fall prey to various religious cults and exotic sects. We will probably go through a phase where it will appear that both new-style spiritual movements and old-style religious fundamentalisms have come to rest in 'secular' Australia. One can catch glimpses of these changes already. Various kinds of literal and sometimes ugly and distorted expressions of the religious impulse arise in the wider community. The police and the mass media smell out these primitive religious stirrings and brand them as satanic practices or demonic rituals. The autonomous religious impulse, acting spontaneously and outside the purview of official religion, is almost always treated by the social superego as lunacy or fraud. A recent Australian weekend magazine that reviewed local occult groups was headed 'Satan in the Suburbs'. In a recent television interview, a Salvation Army admiral condemned the 'spiritual lone rangers and mavericks' in this country who 'acted without the blessing of denominational leaders'. Social authorities have little understanding of and even less sympathy for the spontaneous activities of the newly reawakened soul and spirit.

Unfortunately, the televisual and print media thrives on the negative or inferior expressions of the spontaneous religious impulse. Extreme or bizarre elements in the new cults are sensationalised and are automatically used to damn everything that seems a bit odd, unusual, or out of the ordinary. This has a regressive and stultifying effect upon the spiritual development of the nation, because every time an unconventional religious expression is 'exposed' and undermined this serves only to *reinforce our former ironic and debunking rationalist mode*. Like the well-groomed and morally righteous television presenter, the viewing audience can point to outbreaks of the irrational in the community and say: Look at how appalling, destructive, and inhumane this sort of thing is. Yet the mythopoetic archetypal currents will keep disturbing the uncomprehending surface of society, despite the fact that the public conscience and superego, institutionalised in the mass media, will always attempt to discredit them and to reinstate the controlling rational ego.

There is absolutely no guarantee that the repressed spiritual life of the community will allow itself to be comfortably contained within the existing religious structures. This important problem is further explored in Chapter 9, 'Tracking the Sacred in Secular Society'. It is almost certain that the explosion of the spirit will not lead to an immediate revitalisation of the Church, because by definition the newly arising psychic contents are in opposition to the ruling cultural canon, and at best they will act in a compensatory way to the established religious orthodoxy. The psychological revolution will make spiritual lone rangers and mavericks of many of us, since the new psychic energies cannot be poured into the old religious moulds. The new wine of the spirit will demand new bottles, new labels, and different tastes. The Church will most likely close its doors to the new revelations of the spirit, because its primary task is to defend and support orthodoxy, rather than to chart the course of the wayward spirit. For the Church, religious truth is timeless, absolute, and unchanging, whereas for the living spirit truth is subject to change, relative, and must always be discovered anew.

If Christianity survives the outbreak of spirit, it will be only because individual ministers and priests have realised that the times have changed, and that a new style of religious life is demanded. The living spirit is not particularly concerned with theology, belief, or dogma, but is more concerned with experience and transformation. The future will be gnostic, not theological. Already congregations are warming to priests who emphasise the *experience* of spirit rather than belief in the statements of scripture. The hunger for experience is the hunger of the spirit, and priests and ministers can maintain their flocks only by meeting this hunger, by entering the psychological era and by granting people some inward access to the mysteries of religion. I see this at work in the communities of faith around me: Churches that preach the old news are rapidly declining and losing support, whereas Churches that invite or encourage an inward experience of spirit are at least holding their own. However, positive changes within the official structures cannot keep pace with demands, and this is why spiritualistic Churches, charismatic born-again groups, and revivalist movements are gaining enormous followings. Hardly an empty seat can be found in those 'churches' that convey occult wisdom and telepathic messages to the spiritually starved masses.

As we enter a new age of the spirit, literalism will remain the real and constant danger until a new shared cosmology or religious vision has been achieved. People outside the Church will feel impelled to remythologise the self and the world, but some will get caught up in all manner of ugly literalisms and inappropriate expressions. Instead of ritualising and ensouling daily life, some will act out the religious impulse by participating in black or white magic circles after work. Instead of seeking to develop soulful connections with each other, some will try to create ecstatic communion through naked rituals or orgiastic practices. A sudden experience of a powerful healing archetype is debased and literalised by joining a born-again sect and by endlessly mouthing the clichés of the group. There are *seeds* of genuine truth in all of these warped and vulgar forms of contemporary behaviour, and the task of a future high culture, one that is alert to the reality and power of the spirit, will be to educate the autonomous religious impulse by opposing ugly literalisms and by restoring the spiritual impulse to its symbolic and creative nature. The soul demands a symbolic life, and when the official culture fails to encourage, or disallows, this, the soul will find covert, pathological, and untutored forms of expression. We could almost say that the prevailing secular canon creates pathology and madness in the community, that it puts 'Satan' in the suburbs by failing to provide authentic and legitimate channels for spirit and soul. When there is no religious structure that meets the needs of the community, then one can expect social and psychological disruption until the culture has been reorganised around these pressing needs.

Initially, it may well be easier for us as a nation to approach the task of remythologising and resacralising through environmental and social ecology (further explored in Chapters 8 and 9). After all, ecology almost looks like a pragmatic and secular activity, and devotion to the needs of the environment may not cause the same embarrassment that devotion to the spirit would generate. Through ecology we attend to possibly the most urgent practical issues in the world today, and yet, most surely, behind and within the practice of ecology there is also the romantic and mythopoetic impulse, eros itself, engaged in its vital and ancient task of binding, weaving and connecting us to the other. Through ecology we strive to heal the world and ourselves, to transcend the contemporary alienated condition and to link our souls vitally to the soul of the world. Some may denounce this as a primitive longing, but, call it what you will, the fact remains that the human soul, once it has been activated and released from its slumber in the unconscious, demands connection and will make connections.

7

Black and white Australia

The new experience of Aboriginality: from shadow to shaman

It is at this point in Australia's history that the relationship between Euro-Australians and Aboriginal Australians will be completely reassessed. Since the Aboriginal people have a profound cosmology of place, a living spiritual mythology, which binds them organically to the land,[1] European Australians will look to Aboriginals with tremendous envy and spiritual longing. The values of the past will be reversed: not we superior and they mere shadowy figures upon the floor of hell, but we spiritually barren and they spiritually rich and well endowed. One can observe this dramatic shift everywhere at the present time, but one can find it especially in the middle classes of white suburbia. In archetypal terms, Aboriginals have ceased being carriers of the white person's shadow and have become messengers of the sacred; they are now psychopomps, or personifications of what Jung calls the Self. When the early colonial consciousness is menaced by the psychic depths, the indigenous people are seen as negative; when the postcolonial ego needs to be transformed and looks to the unconscious for reconciliation and healing, Aboriginals are experienced as spiritual guides. From loathsome, hostile primitives to carriers of our own shamanic transformation: that is the crucial change now taking place in our mythic apperception of Aboriginal people.

Although this change represents a shift from negative to positive attitudes, there is no reason to suppose that either the shadow or the shamanic perspective affords a real connection with Aboriginal people. We have simply moved from one archetypal projection to another, since Aboriginality itself is not merely a creation derived from psychic contents of the white psyche; it is not merely a white person's fantasy. We need to be alert to the fact that the more positive recent image comes not as a result of a genuine change of heart about indigenous people, but from a response to our own need to befriend the deeper, more primal or 'aboriginal' layer in our own psychic structure. This deeper, spiritual layer in ourselves is now being projected upon Aboriginal people, and this gives rise to several important cultural problems.

The first I have already alluded to: if Aboriginality equals spirituality, then we have not really seen the Aboriginal people at all. We continue in our old mode of foisting psychological projections upon them. Rather than understanding Aboriginals as a complex people, we reduce them to a single archetype, which can so rapidly turn into an imprisoning stereotype. This means that they are not respected as a real people with real material and developmental needs, but viewed as participants in a desert fairytale: they remain disembodied, outside history and material reality, and outside our real concern. Secretly, we may even hope that they remain materially impoverished and politically disempowered, because this better accords with our own split-off, disincarnate and otherworldly conception of the sacred. Aboriginals ought to be free to live their Dreaming *and* to move toward political independence and material prosperity. Spirituality ought not be regarded as antithetical to worldliness, and in this regard the New Zealand example has much to teach us. The Maori cultural renaissance is working toward both a revival of traditional spirituality and the achievement of political power and economic security.

Secondly, by projecting sacredness upon Aboriginals, white Australians disempower themselves spiritually and refuse to accept responsibility for their own souls. Euro-Australians have made a national pastime of self-flagellation and self-revilement. For many years it was the British to whom we felt subordinate, and this gave rise to what Arthur Phillips called the cultural cringe.[2] After the Second World War it was the Americans to whom we were supposed to feel inferior. I grew up with the awareness that we were always following the American model and doomed perpetually to be ten to fifteen years 'behind' them. Now, in another era, the Australian middle classes and the new age fringe-dwellers join together in the indulgent experience of feeling inferior to Aboriginal people. Alongside Aboriginals, many Euro-Australians feel themselves to be merely ego, merely material, empty and hollow. We have given over to Aboriginals our own unconscious soul, and stand bereft, disempowered, impoverished. We have become the sad-sack, down-in-the-mouth alienated ego, and they the very personification of the sacred, vibrantly and organically connected with nature and bonded with the spirit of the earth.

In his poem 'The Inverse Transports', Les Murray addresses several of these contemporary concerns. In particular, he explores the dangers in recent white attitudes:

> but fairytale is a reserve, for those rich only
> in that and fifty thousand years here.
> The incomers will acquire those fifty thousand
> years too, though. Thousands of anything
> draw them. They discovered thousands,
> even these. Which they offer now, for settlement.[3]

The popular mind has made Aboriginals the sole curators of imaginal reality: the mythopoetic world has become a 'fairytale reserve' enjoyed only by those who are poor but rich. No money, but they have 'thousands' of years. The very concept of thousands of years, as Murray says, is a white person's construct. We offer these thousands for settlement. I recall as a youth that the stated period of Aboriginal occupancy of the land was ten thousand years. Then it jumped to forty thousand, where it remained for some time. Now the figure is fifty thousand. The period of time offered by modern science increases in exact proportion to white guilt, and to a need to invest spiritual value in the Aboriginal other. Les Murray has correctly perceived what was to be my next major point: so long as Euro-Australians project their soul upon Aboriginal people we will want it back from them again. 'The incomers will acquire those fifty thousand / years too, though. Thousands of anything / draw them'. This is the real 'catch' to the contemporary idealisation of Aboriginal people. If the sacred has become neatly embodied in the indigenous people, then the Western consumerist mentality will want to devour and consume Aboriginality. We already see this all around us: in the thriving business spawned by the trendy 'Aboriginal' art and souvenir shops in the hearts of our cities, in the better suburbs, and in airport lounges. We buy up the works of art and the commercially reproduced symbols and designs, hoping thereby to enrich our souls with Aboriginal experiences of the sacred. Thus, it could be said that in the recent past we have made Aboriginality more 'positive' in order to make a more delectable and tasty meal out of it. By an elaborate process of projective identification, we prettify and adorn what we are about to consume.

The consuming of Aboriginal cosmology is merely the most recent expression of the white imperialist appropriation of the indigenous other. We have not only stolen Aboriginal land, destroyed the tribal culture, raped the women and the environment, but we now ask for their spirituality as well. We ask for their Dreaming because, as W.E.H. Stanner has put it, 'White Man Got No Dreaming'.[4] Given the facts about what has transpired so far between whites and blacks in this country it is hardly surprising that our pursuit of Aboriginal cosmology is read by many political commentators as still further evidence of our wilful destruction of this ancient culture.[5]

Finally, there are other psychospiritual and cultural problems here. Euro-Australians cannot simply graft onto their own souls a fifty-thousand-year-old Dreaming borrowed or stolen from another tradition. Such a borrowing would not necessarily take root in the white soul, and might in fact inhibit or block a developmental process already taking place there. We know we are spiritually bereft, but the way ahead may not be by means of a return to archaic animism and a belief in ancestor spirits. For the Western psyche, this may simply represent a regression to a spiritistic world-view, which predates modernity and which would engender enormous tension between the soul and our developed intellect. Our need is certainly to remythologise and to develop spiritual kinship with the land, but the Aboriginal cosmology may best serve us as an inspiration to create our own cosmology, rather than as a template or foundation upon which to build our own. We need to regard Aboriginal mysteries metaphorically rather than literally, to experience them as rich cultural fantasies that stir our own souls to activity, rather than as metaphysical systems to believe in.

What is needed is a spiritual revolution in Euro-Australian consciousness. We cannot merely tack on Aboriginal spirituality to our own faulty or overly-rational consciousness, but must change our consciousness from within by burrowing down into our feared and previously walled-in unconscious in order to find, or create, an answering image to Aboriginal spirituality. The direction we need to take is downward, into our own depths, to see what could be happening there, rather than to remain the same and move sideways by appropriating another culture's dreaming. Jung wrote that 'People will do anything, no matter how absurd, in order to avoid facing their own souls'.[6] It is far easier, he said, to take on the spirituality of a foreign culture, to wrap our nakedness in the wondrous trappings of an exotic cosmology, than it is to face the apparent poverty of our own souls and to begin a real dialogue with the unconscious inner life of which we are at present oblivious. We will have to risk an encounter with the other within ourselves, whatever the cost to our much-vaunted rationality and whatever the long-term impact upon our hubristic consciousness.

The activation of the 'indigenous' archetype

It may also be the case that white Australians have begun to be 'aboriginalised' from within, in ways that we have still to realise. In his intriguing essay 'Mind and Earth', Jung writes:

> Certain Australian Aborigines assert that one cannot conquer foreign soil, because in it there dwell strange ancestor-spirits who reincarnate themselves in the new-born. There is a great psychological truth in this. The foreign land assimilates its conqueror.[7]

The present book has been largely concerned with the process of colonisation-in-reverse, with the process by which the new-old land has assimilated its conqueror. This process could readily be extended to include the idea that the conqueror 'becomes' or takes on the likeness of those who have been conquered. Although not drawn by the idea of the transmigration of 'ancestor-spirits', Jung does speculate that the 'earth' seems to exert a power over 'mind', and in his own terms this has something to do with the direct link between the deep unconscious and the world of nature. The deep world of the psyche, which is really 'nature' inside us, is directly influenced by the forces of nature 'outside' us. In Australia, where land and Aboriginality are fused, this means that white Australians, virtually in spite of themselves, are slowly aboriginalised in their unconscious.

Jung's writings on the subject of 'mind and earth' are primarily concerned with the North American situation, but there is that important reference to the Australian experience. This whole topic about the relationship between mind and earth is an intuitive subject, and I am not even going to pretend to dress it up, as Jung did, as pseudo-science. I think the idea that earth impacts on psyche is a mythopoetic claim, which cannot be scientifically proved or disproved. Many would therefore reject it as baseless, but I don't follow this way of thinking; I am inclined to take the claim very seriously, even if it seems irrational. It may not be good science, but it is good myth, and that is what interests and sustains me.

White Australians come into contact with Aboriginal figures in their dreams, more than in reality. I have always been amazed at the number of urban Australians who have major dreams about Aboriginals; often these dreams involve important symbols of initiation, or ritual movements and dances. I know that I have had numerous 'big' dreams involving Aboriginal figures and motifs, and that I had most of these dreams after I had left the outback and was living in safe suburbs. Aboriginals are *significant archetypal others* for white Australians: in some dreams they are quite obviously shadow-figures, who stalk, worry and interfere with the ego personality, but in other dreams they tend to present as black shamans or priests who lead the ego into various kinds of spiritual initiation. If we take dreams and archetypal processes seriously, then we can certainly agree with Jung that the white psyche is being Aboriginalised from within. In *Kangaroo* D.H. Lawrence claimed that a psychic connection between the two cultures seemed evident, but it was largely unconscious and difficult to conceptualise. Anyway, the process was real enough to scare Lawrence away from these shores: he said he could not physically bear to be connected with such an archaic level of primitive life.

Many Australian artists have been alert to a process of 'aboriginalisation' within the white Australian psyche. Judith Wright, Roland Robinson and the Jindyworobak poets,[8] Les Murray, Rodney Hall, and numerous others have explored this theme in their work. In popular art and sculpture, William Ricketts has done much to impress upon Australians that the soul of this country is profoundly Aboriginal. Murray has written numerous poems on this theme, as well as several prose essays, including 'The Human Hair Thread', and 'Some Religious Stuff I Know about Australia'. None of these artists need refer to Jung or Lawrence to make their point: they have the authority of their own imagination to go by, and their work tells them that there is a meeting of cultures in the psychic depths. None of these artists is perturbed by the new intellectual view that Aboriginality is off limits, and that to deal with it as a spiritual reality is the last and probably the most unacceptable sign of Western cultural imperialism. It is the rational intellect that comes up with these objections, whereas in the intuitive depths of this country's psyche, contact between whites and blacks has already occurred and no ideological barriers can put a stop to it.

This controversial theme may be made less controversial if we attempt to deliteralise what we mean by the term 'aboriginalisation'. Here we may be helped by the contemporary black African writer, Malidoma Some, who argues that there is an indigenous archetype within the collective human psyche. In his book *Ritual*, Some tells his American audience: 'There is an indigenous person within each of us. The indigenous archetype within the modern soul is in serious need of acknowledgment. A different set of priorities dwells there, a set of priorities long forgotten in Western society'.[9] This 'indigenous archetype' can express itself in us in various ways: in my case it links me indirectly to Aboriginality, in the case of others it might link them to Celtic or Jewish sources. The important thing to bear in mind is that there is not just one way of activating indigeneity within the modern soul. The impact or 'influence' of Aboriginality upon the white psyche is subtle and complex—and it is psychological rather than metaphysical. *Whatever 'latent' layer of indigenous life lies buried beneath the sophisticated ego will be stirred to activity by the mythopoetic power and resonance of Aboriginal culture* (this will be further explored in the next chapter, in relation to the work of Rodney Hall). In animistic language, this is how the 'strange ancestor-spirits *reincarnate* themselves in the new-born'. Whatever equates with Aboriginality in the unconsious of Westerners will be mobilised in the Australian experience. In any event, resacralisation in this country will be a complex phenomenon, since in a multicultural, multiracial society there will be many parallel tracks upon which this process will run. Malidoma Some's advice is wonderfully insightful, and I am glad that a black writer said it, because a white person could readily be accused of cultural imperialism and exploitation.

I firmly believe that the 'acknowledgement' that Malidoma Some is talking about is what is needed in Australian society. Whites here need to acknowledge the indigenous archetype within themselves, to be better related to the 50 000-year-old man or woman inside us. The process of resacralisation in this country will undoubtedly prove to be synonymous with the activation of the indigenous archetypal other. The suburban dreams about Aboriginal shamans and guides show us that the unconscious is already trying to force the 'indigenous' soul upon white consciousness, but all too often this new awakening remains merely at the level of symbolic possibility or mythic suggestion, in which case there is in the Australian psyche a frustration of archetypal intent. In this psychological sense, the new Mabo legislation could almost be read as a defensive and legalistic acting-out of an impulse which is refused realisation at a deeper and more challenging level. It is relatively easy to construct piles of government documents and unreadable official prose in order to fob off or deny the more difficult claims that are being made by the interior indigenous archetypal person.

Aboriginal culture in transition: expulsion from the maternal round

> We are nature and the past, all the old ways
> Gone now and scattered.
> — OODGEROO OF THE TRIBE NOONUCCAL[10]
> (formerly Kath Walker)

It appears that there is also significant spiritual change on the other side of the cultural divide in Australia. As a non-Aboriginal I am unable to speak with authority on the situation of the Aboriginal psyche, but as someone who grew up and worked with Aboriginal people for a significant period of time, I feel I can make some comment on this topic. It seems to me that Aboriginal people are experiencing a psychocultural development that is virtually the reverse of what Euro-Australians are going through.[11] The Western psyche has overdosed on patriarchal spirit (the Logos, or Word) and now needs to make an urgent turn toward maternal nature and the mysteries of the earth. The Aboriginal people, on the other hand, have long been children of the Earth Mother, and have been nourished and contained by the archetypal field of nature for millennia. This is not to deny that Aboriginal culture has 'developed' in the course of time: the anthropological literature indicates that it has been far from a static culture,[12] although it can appear so to the untrained eye. However, from an archetypal perspective, the changes have taken place within the context of an overall subordination to the earth mother. Although there are clear indications of social and political patriarchy within the structure of Aboriginal society, the actual archetypal situation is matriarchal and is governed by the laws of nature.[13]

Life governed by the earth mother is life lived within the maternal round. We know from comparative studies of ancient mythologies and symbol systems that the perfect circle is a primary symbol of this archetypal situation.[14] The earth mother encloses everything within her cosmic embrace: she is mistress of life, death, rebirth, and the natural mysteries. In this condition, there is a sense of spiritual harmony between humanity and nature; there is an almost Edenic relationship between all living beings. Humanity is not divorced from nature but part of nature, and the creatures of the earth are perceived as spirit-cousins of humankind. There is very often in this situation a sense of psychic continuity between animals and humans, a symbiotic connection throughout the natural world, and sometimes (as in the Aboriginal 'bush telegraph') a remarkable form of intuitive communication between human beings similar to what we would call extrasensory perception. Everything is co-ordinated in an 'ecologically sound' way, but this is not an ecology that is arrived at by deliberation and planning; rather, it is the natural shape of existence so long as everything is kept inside the symbolic maternal circle.

If something contrary to the dictates of nature wants to enter this primordial harmony there will be terrible strife. If an archetypal principle that is essentially different from the earth mother and threatening to her divine power wants to be born, this will be resisted bitterly by the mother, who wants to maintain her sovereignty above all else.[15] She maintains her position best by keeping humanity dependent upon her, in other words, by ensuring that human beings remain her 'children' and eternally indebted to her providence. Ancient mythologies, especially pre-Christian mythologies, are full of examples of this sort of symbiotic relationship between humanity and the Earth Mother.[16] To break out of this maternal circle is constructed as a crime against nature and the natural order of things. Hence, despite social and political changes within these primal societies, the overall condition is strictly conservative and archetypally fixed. The price paid, so to speak, for such primal harmony and perfection, is psychological rigidity and a life-style prescribed by a whole series of collectivist and religious taboos. The primordial connectedness to the earth has many emotional and spiritual advantages, but also many severe drawbacks and limitations, especially insofar as the development of the individual self is concerned. It is essential that the ambivalent aspect of this mythological mode is pointed out, both for the sake of romantic whites who strive to idealise it, and for nostalgic Aboriginal artists who represent the past as a golden age, which must be recaptured and returned to in the future.

In Judeo-Christian myth, the primal cosmic parent is constructed as a Father God who has created an idyllic world for humanity, so long as primary taboos are not broken and so long as humanity does not begin to question the paradisal situation in which it finds itself. In Jungian terms, the presiding archetype will offer paradisal harmony and unity, provided humanity is content to remain subordinate to the archetype in a state of near-unconsciousness. The desire to find out more about the world is constructed as the original sin, inspired by the devil himself. The serpent tempts Eve to taste of the tree of knowledge of good and evil, which symbolises the primal opposites that will split apart the condition of unconscious unity. If humans taste of the fruit, they will become like Gods, knowing good and evil. In other words, they will have transcended the primal innocent condition, and gain access to a different consciousness. Unconscious containment within the archetype is always presented as the divinely ordained or 'right' condition, and the desire for increased knowledge or broader awareness is presented as a 'fall' from the state of grace. These two elements are generally at war in world mythologies, as they are also at war within each human heart. The impulse to conform is matched by the desire to rebel; subservience to the God is matched by the longing to become God-like in a bid for greater consciousness.

No-one would wish to underestimate the devastating impact that European colonisation has had upon the Aboriginal people. The colonisation of this country was carried out with violence, imperialistic aggression, and widespread insensitivity to indigenous rights, values, and culture. For two hundred years Euro-Australians have undermined and attacked—literally and morally— Aboriginal society, and the new 'idealisation' of Aboriginality is a relatively recent phenomenon, which has still to yield positive effects. Nevertheless—and not wishing to 'excuse' white Australians for the atrocities of the past— it may be possible to see something potentially creative and transformative in this tragic clash of cultures. It could well be that, at an archetypal level, white intrusion into the primal round of Aboriginality is a profoundly significant symbolic event. In other words, there could be a meaningful synchronicity to the clash of white and black in Australia. Although mostly we are aware of the negative side of this intrusion, or invasion, it could prove to be very much more than just a political take-over and cultural tragedy. The puncturing of the circle could be seen in a larger sense as the intrusion of a progressive spirit that had to arrive in the Aboriginal psyche in one form or another. Either the primal embrace would be dissolved by internal psycho-mythological change, or it would be rudely interrupted by the intrusion of a different race—whether by the British or any other nation is incidental from this larger mythic standpoint. It may be that there was something new already stirring in the Aboriginal psyche, a spirit that had been excluded from the paradisal Garden, and that since this spirit could not easily find its way into the psyche while the earth mother continued her reign, the intrusion was enacted externally, and almost fatally, as political fate.

A universal fact common to all peoples of the world is that Edenic oneness with nature cannot last forever or be infinitely sustained. There is an opposite, contrary force at work in the human psyche, usually symbolised as masculine and patriarchal, that works against nature to create a separate realm of logos or spirit. The symbolism of this intruding moment ranges from satanic interruption, to loss of innocence, to rape or abduction, to sudden onset of chaos and havoc. However brutal or dreadful this moment appears, it is sometimes retrospectively regarded as the necessary evil (*felix culpa*) that would bring on an entirely new phase of consciousness and the promise of future development. In my reading of contemporary Aboriginal writing, I am struck by the strongly mythological images and associations relating to the portrayal of white people in Australia. In the more emotive protest writings, whites are sometimes seen as serpents invading the innocent shores of Australia, as vermin, filth, sorcerers, and bringers of darkness and corruption.[17] As Mudrooroo Narogin (Colin Johnson) has written, in Aboriginal writing 'Europeans intrude into the pristine world of Australia as an evil disrupting force'.[18] While I am sure that some of this imagery is realistically justified, the overall impact on me is that a huge mythological force is constellated here: an alien archetypal power is portrayed in a demonic and satanic light, and we know from mythology that this heralds the end of one state of being and the beginning of another age. What the new age will bring is difficult to determine at this stage, and there is still a great deal of mourning, loss, and tragedy to be experienced before the new mythological dispensation can clearly emerge.

As a youth in Alice Springs in the 1960s I was moved by the Aboriginal paintings of mandalas that revealed one side of the protective circle blown to pieces by a mysterious force, with precious contents previously contained by the circle spilling out of the gaping wound. It was evident that there had been a deep injury to the indigenous psyche, although at the time I had no way of knowing what the broken circle could mean. Jungian psychology allows us to see the broken mandalas as the shattering of a primal condition of unity, giving rise to much psychic pain, to disorientation, suffering, and a deep nostalgia for life prior to this disruption. It is perhaps cold comfort to point out that the disrupted mandala is also a moment of growth, a painful crisis that brings with it the possibility of transformation and redemption. A new archetypal force has entered the ancient mythological precinct and torn open the sacred maternal round, which symbolises the mystic unity with the earth and the mother.

The devastating impact of a unity-puncturing spirit could well throw some psychological light on the increasing and urgent problem of alcoholism in the Aboriginal community. 'Alcohol' in Latin is *spiritus*, and the destructiveness of alcohol could symbolise, at a bodily and somatic level, the invasive and disorienting effect of the spirit archetype upon a people traditionally contained within the sacred precinct of nature. What is not integrated in the psyche is often, according to Jung, somatised in the body and experienced as bodily disease or substance abuse. Unintegrated spirit is not only able to unbalance the psyche, but, at a lower level, it can actually poison the body. As Jung wrote to the co-founder of Alcoholics Anonymous: '"alcohol" in Latin is *spiritus*, and one uses the same word for the highest religious experience as well as for the most depraving poison. The helpful formula therefore is: *spiritus contra spiritum*'.[19]

Jung means by this last cryptic phrase that only the spirit archetype can effect a cure upon diseases of spirit. Like cures like—or more precisely, like takes away the symptoms of like—and this is actually the philosophical basis of traditional homeopathic medicine. One employs a higher or more distilled form of the poison to combat the poison. In the case of Aboriginal alcoholism, only a higher integration of the archetypal spirit—and an integration of the meaning of its shattering disruption of primal unity— can calm the chaos wrought by the low-level ingestion of intoxicating fluids. Alcohol is a perfect symbol of the alien spirit, since this intoxicant was apparently unknown here until imported by Europeans, and apparently the Aboriginal metabolism cannot break down or 'digest' this substance in the way that other cultural groups can, hence drunkenness or intolerance to the liquid occurs more readily. In its unintegrated or undigested state, archetypal spirit—like its bottled namesake—is a fatal agent of ruin and degradation. When living in Alice Springs I was always impressed by the fact that those Aboriginals who had best learnt to overcome alcoholism were those who had made a firm personal conversion to a religious faith. Although some claim that religion is the 'opium of the masses', its capacity to provide a creative channel for the unruly and chaotic spirit cannot be underestimated.

An archetypal assault by spirit is extremely difficult to integrate when individual and cultural esteem is low and human integrity threatened. The growth potential of the present crisis is currently overshadowed by the misery of dismemberment and the pain of loss. The expectation that Aboriginal people should 'assimilate' to white culture is completely misguided, since the white condition of psychic alienation from nature would prove not only unattractive but also fatal to a people who have drawn their very life-blood from the archetypal Earth Mother for several millennia. Aboriginals should not be expected to suddenly adopt the white archetypal position, but should be allowed to develop their own psychocultural style at their own pace. What they end up discovering could well be of enormous value to Euro-Australians and to the rest of the world, since an integration of nature and spirit is the precious formula that the world needs at this critical time of environmental degradation and spiritual crisis.

Clearly, a mythology that accommodates rupture and a wounding of the primal cosmic round will have to be discovered or invented. What is demanded is a strategic reorganisation of the cultural psyche based upon a new wholeness that is able to sustain conflict, opposition, and the 'invasion' of the transformative spirit. A major obstacle to this development is the character of traditional mythology, which has always been a mythology of belonging, not of exile and disruption. Contemporary Aboriginals are in exile not only from their traditional lands but from a unitary reality that will probably never be recovered in the same way. Here is a vital and important role for contemporary Aboriginal art and writing: the construction of new mythologies and images of wholeness, which can create a new kind of psychic equilibrium, one which postdates the archetypal invasion and the breaking of the original cosmic mandala. The writings of Mudrooroo are especially important in this context, since they point to the possibility of a new kind of personal and cultural wholeness that allows spiritual fellowship with the earth as well as acceptance of the radically different world that Aboriginals now inhabit.[20] His spirituality has certain elements in common with the traditional dreaming, only it accepts contemporary conditions and the new order of things, it acknowledges the rupture that has occurred, and it views this rupture optimistically as an opening to new mythic possibilites rather than as a death-blow to the culture. In *Master of the Ghost Dreaming* we read: 'Now, we, the pitiful fragments of once strong families suffer on in exile ... All around us is the darkness of the night; all around us is an underlying silence of a land of death ... We are in despair; we are sickening unto death; we call to be healed. We demand healing from our shaman, who can sing the way of release through song ...'[21] Importantly, although his writings often point to the lost unity of the ancient past they do not hanker nostalgically or painfully after that past, but instead use it as a source of integrity and strength, which can come to the support of the contemporary quest for a new spiritual dispensation.

One hopes that white Australians will become sensitive to the crucial changes and deep structural reorientation occurring within the Aboriginal world. However, on a more cynical note, it probably serves contemporary white society best to continue to view Aboriginals as Noble Savages held in the primal Edenic embrace of the earth mother, since this is the fantasy-ideal that Euro-Australians look for at the moment, as they make their own nostalgic and guilt-ridden return to the realm of the mother. White Australians may not appreciate the new development within Aboriginality, because they seem to need to believe in the fantasy of an indigenous people blissfully at one with the earth in order to take them out of their habitual heroic and alienated mode, and to inspire them on a new course, which will involve spiritual connection with nature.

Whites and blacks are moving in opposite psycho-cultural directions, which is why it is so difficult to achieve any mutual understanding at this stage. Whites, brutally and perilously over-sophisticated, are idealising nature and heading that way. Blacks, for so long in the primal round, are now impelled toward a new development, while also needing to maintain their psychical identity with the earth. (As Oodgeroo Noonuccal writes: 'Let none tell me the past is wholly gone'.[22]) Perhaps we will meet each other in the middle, as we cross our new cultural paths. It is an extremely exciting time, and there is much that each group can learn from the other, as each stands at the edge of a new experience of the sacred.

8

Toward a new dreaming

Our task is to enter into the dream of Nature.

— GRANT WATSON[1]

Animism versus rationality: the clash of two stories

The Aboriginal Dreaming and Western rationality stand to each other as thesis to antithesis. What the one affirms, the other denies. In Aboriginal cosmology, landscape is a living field of spirits and metaphysical forces. The earth is animated by ancestral creator-beings who engaged in primal rituals at the dawn of time and whose spirits fused with the earth to shape, form, and sacralise it. Landscape is a mytho-spiritual field which acts upon human beings from without, causing them to conform to ancient patterns and to re-enact the lives and movements of ancestral animals and other beings. Landscape is at the centre of everything: at once the source of life, the origin of the tribe, the metamorphosed body of blood-line ancestors, and the intelligent force that drives the individual and creates society.[2] As Judith Wright has pointed out, our English word 'landscape' is wholly inadequate to describe the 'earth–sky–water–tree–spirit–human continuum'[3] which is the cosmological and existential ground of the Aboriginal Dreaming.

For contemporary Western consciousness landscape is barren, empty, unalive. Far from being animated by ancient spirits of place, landscape is seen as a dead objective background to our busy, ego-centred and self-propelling human lives. For us, human beings are moved not by primordial earth-spirits, but by society, conditioning, and subjective impulses. Always in the Western frame subjectivity is privileged and regarded as the ruling element. If the landscape is felt to possess a certain character or mood, then this is said to be created by the perceiving subject and *projected* upon the land. Freud said that the primal view of an animated natural world 'is nothing but psychology projected into the external world'.[4] Western intellectual tradition has a host of terms and concepts to explain away any attempt to animate the land in life or art: projection, personification, anthropomorphism, pathetic fallacy. Any life 'out there' was *put* there by an overactive or 'creative' mind. Indeed, the contemporary postmodern view is not even sure that there is a real landscape at all, or whether our experience of the land is entirely created by our own subjectivity.[5] All we can know, according to this bleak intellectualist position, are our own internal images, which we project vainly upon the world.

We are faced with two completely different and competing stories about the same Australian earth. In the one, objectivity reigns supreme; in the other, subjectivity is all. In the old story, individuals are relatively powerless in the face of archaic spiritual energies, which co-ordinate and control reality. In the new story, the individual is invested with god-like powers in the sense that the subject creates the world in the act of apprehending it. As Wright makes clear, the imported Western story has subsumed, engulfed and discredited the indigenous one:

The song is gone ...
... and the tribal story
lost in an alien tale.[6]

In the past, Euro-Australians have viewed the Aboriginal world-picture as weird, bizarre, and hopelessly unrealistic. Yet surely, if we look upon both from a distance, the animistic Aboriginal view, which focuses upon an objective unseen reality, is not a bit more bizarre than the Western subjectivist view, with its grotesque inflation of the perceiving subject and its refusal to grant autonomous psychic reality to the larger universe. Judith Wright is accurate in describing ours as an 'alien' tale. Although our story grants god-like powers to the individual, the individual actually feels not super-human but sub-human in the postmodern world. A sense of almost complete unreality and alienation plagues contemporary life. We feel isolated, lonely, rootless, disconnected. Nature is at best a dead background to our human endeavours, at worst a surreal or nightmare projection from our own heads. This alienation is hardly a recent phenomenon, but is a culmination of a long historical process in Western European cultures.

The necessity of re-enchantment

> It is difficult to undo our own damage, and to recall to our presence that which we have asked to leave. It is hard to desecrate a sacred grove and change your mind … We doused the burning bush and cannot rekindle it; we are lighting matches in vain under every green tree. Did the wind once cry, and the hills shout forth praise? Now speech has perished from among the lifeless things of earth, and living things say very little to very few.
>
> — ANNJE DILLARD[7]

At least since the beginning of the patriarchal era, humanity has sought to differentiate itself from nature and to know itself as distinct from nature. The human spirit has soared above the natural world, and the very core of the Judeo-

Christian religion is a celebration of the triumph of spirit over nature. This separation has made possible a highly developed cerebral consciousness and a strong self-awareness that probably would not have evolved had we remained in a state of emotional identity with nature. But we have gone far enough along this heroic course. The cost of our excessive differentiation from the natural world is painfully apparent to everyone and now threatens the very existence of the human and biological sphere. Our overzealous heroic exploits and our patriarchal abuses of the maternal earth must be stopped, and humanity must immediately find a new pact or bond with nature.

How can the new bond be forged? I have grave doubts about the effectiveness of 'progressive' governments and ecology groups simply telling people to care more about the environment. In the present environmental crisis, moral demands and appeals to collective guilt about what we have done to the landscape may serve short-term goals; we may have to be frightened into some kind of new bond or relationship with nature. But for the long term we will not only have to stir our conscience, but also *transform our consciousness*. The ecological crisis is at bottom a psychological and spiritual crisis. These deeper roots to the problem will have to be explored if there is to be any lasting change.[8]

Oodgeroo Noonuccal wrote: 'White fellow, you are the unhappy race. / You alone have left nature and made civilised laws'.[9] We can no longer afford to be so deeply divorced from nature, but somehow nature will have to be experienced in a new way, as *part* of our larger spiritual and psychological being. Aboriginal people have long been an ecologically committed people, not because they laboured, like us today, under moral constraints about what they must do or feel about the environment, but because they spontaneously felt the environment to be part of themselves and to be intrinsically related to their emotional reality. This is the missing dimension in today's official discourse about the necessity to be green. The secular and purely moral approach to this problem simply will not work, because the issues are deeper than most activist programmes will allow. The rationalist mindset is itself part of the problem, and it cannot be expected to come up with a cure.

Human love moves toward that with which it can identify, to that which it sees as part of itself. Affective bonds unite us with 'our' family, 'our' home and 'our' concerns. There needs to be a fundamental shift in the *locus* of identity, so that what we care about, and what we regard as belonging to ourselves, is radically broadened so as to accommodate a far greater span or portion of reality. Put cynically, if humans care only about themselves, then the notion of what constitutes 'self' has to be totally transformed and broadened in the direction of the world. The truly ecological task is not only to repair our damage in the outer world, but to repair the deep splits on the inside, to work toward inclusive rather than exclusive concepts of selfhood and identity.

The desired change can come about only by way of a fundamental re-enchantment of the world. As I have indicated, early man's experience of nature as a field of enchantment and animation was quite spontaneous and even automatic. Anthropologist Levy-Bruhl argued that tribal man is involved in a state of mystical participation (French: 'participation mystique') with the environment.[10] This is the natural and normal state of affairs for early man, and the condition of 'participation mystique' is hardly unique to Aboriginals, but is found throughout the world in premodern times, as well as in contemporary tribal societies. We will have to attempt to recover something similar to that early primal vision. We will have to make some kind of return to the past in order to reanimate the world and ourselves. But I believe we will recover the old primal vision in an entirely new way. D.H. Lawrence put it best when he said that we need to make a 'detour' back toward the primal state in order to revitalise and invigorate civilisation: 'We must make a great swerve in our onward-going life-course now, to gather up again the savage mysteries'. Lawrence insisted that this is not tantamount to a full-blown cultural regression, but is a return in the service of civilisation: 'But this does not mean going back on ourselves. We can't go back'.[11]

Lawrence's idea that we need to make a 'great swerve' toward the primal condition makes enormous sense to me. This may look like mere regression from a rationalistic perspective, but the idea of a great swerve suggests a spiralic course rather than a straight regression. At the turn of the cultural spiral we will seem to be throwing away the hard-won benefits of differentiated consciousness and advanced civilisation, but it will be apparent that this (re)turn is for the sake of a more integrated consciousness. We will not have to renounce intellect and stifle ego-development, but must simply place less emphasis on these elements of our psychic life as we revisit and embrace the overshadowed, primal side of human nature. Not for ordinary 'ego-development' do we make this journey, but for spiritual development: for soul resides in the deeper levels of psyche, those same levels that we believe we have outgrown.

There are numerous ways in which to construct a theoretical frame for where we are now, how we got here, and what we have to do in order to reanimate the world. Theology,[12] new science,[13] sociology,[14] gnosticism,[15] cosmology[16]— all have begun to develop possibilities for a cultural and spiritual revival, for a process of re-enchantment. The need for some kind of re-enchantment has also been an issue in Jungian depth psychology, to which I will now briefly turn.

Depth psychology and the return of anima(tion) to the world

According to Jung, the Intellectual Enlightenment, which drained the world of its psychic or spiritual content and located *psyche* only within the human being, was an important step in the history of consciousness. It was the stage in which religion was replaced by humanism, and in which myth and magic were gradually dislodged by the sciences. Western scientific progress, Jung said, completely 'despiritualised nature through its so-called objective knowledge of matter', and 'man's [humanity's] mystical identity with nature was curtailed as never before'. Jung argues that the consolation prize was man's discovery of an enormous psychic realm within his own being, so that instead of the pagan gods of nature 'there was disclosed the inner wealth of the soul which lies in every man's [human] heart'.[17]

However, it is a great tragedy that the human psyche could only be discovered by first destroying or denying the spiritual essence of the greater world, almost as if we in the West were so attached to the world that we had to kill it off before we could come to ourselves. The catch to the humanist revolution is that as the world dies spiritually, then physically, as a result of this great withdrawal of psychic energy, the human soul itself withers and dies along with the world. Humanity itself is threatened because the soulful and living dimension of human beings is dependent, in turn, upon the spirituality of nature. Hence, as Jung was well aware, the 'enlightened' psychologistic era cannot last very long, because the human soul, which is that portion of the world-soul located within human beings, cannot stand this deadening confinement and this nullifying constriction. 'Only the individual consciousness that has lost its connection with the psychic totality remains caught in the illusion that the soul is a small circumscribed area, a fit subject for 'scientific' theorising. The loss of this great relationship is the prime evil of neurosis.'[18]

Although Jung was, with Freud, one of the great founders of depth psychology, he seemed very conscious that depth psychology was doomed if it attempted to compartmentalise the psyche into a small box marked 'human subjectivity'. Indeed, the entire thrust of Jung's research was to extend the psyche temporally and spatially into culture, history, and nature. Below the personal unconscious was an objective psychic realm, a world of instincts and archetypes, and at its very deepest level, psyche simply was, or merged into, nature (this level was designated by the term 'psychoid'). After his separation from the Freudian school, Jung moved further and further away from the psychologistic world-view, which wanted continually to reduce everything to human subjectivity. Jung became more impressed by the objective dimension of psychic experience: although we felt psyche to be 'inside' us, psyche (as in soul) revealed itself as a cosmos in its own right. Jung greatly valued ancient philosophical traditions because of their keen perception of the objectivity of the soul. One of Jung's favourite aphorisms came from Heraclitus: 'You could not discover the limits of the soul, even if you travelled every road to do so; such is the depth of its meaning'. He also quoted Sendivogius: 'The greater part of the soul is outside the body'.

In the previous chapter we briefly reviewed Jung's idea that place or earth can exert significant influence upon human nature and behaviour. In a letter of 1943, Jung wrote: 'I am deeply convinced of the—unfortunately—still very mysterious relation between man and landscape'.[19] While Freud seemed convinced that the mythopoetic world-view could be reduced to infantile projections, Jung was moving steadily in the opposite direction: psychology itself was giving way to a reanimated sense of a living cosmos.

Jung also felt that the condition of 'participation mystique' with the environment still persisted beneath the surface of contemporary consciousness, and that its reality and effectiveness could still be felt today whenever our superficial education was stripped away or eroded by the unconscious. Animistic vision and intuitive interaction with the world could still be found in art and poetry, in psychotic states, in dreams, visions, and other spontaneous eruptions of unconscious life. Jung felt that this deeper, primal perception should not be culturally repressed, but should be explored for its potential to revitalise our sterile world. 'Everything old in our unconscious,' he wrote, 'hints at something coming.' [20]

Jung's late theory of synchronicity, which posited a meaningful 'acausal' relationship between human subjectivity and events in the world, was predicated on the assumption of a psychic continuity between inner and outer reality. The theory of an acausal connecting principle made Jung intensely alert to the findings of the new physics, which posited a relationship between observer and observed, and which exploded the old mechanistic understanding of matter in preference for a new, dynamic, processual and interactive view of material reality. He was moved to suggest that 'since psyche and matter ... are in continuous contact with one another, it is not only possible but fairly probable that psyche and matter are two different aspects of one and the same thing'.[21] Jung himself was not far from postulating a kind of postmodern animism, and his efforts in this regard were later taken up by James Hillman.

Hillman, writing in an ecological era which post-dated Jung's world, was quick to seize upon the connections between Jung's theorising and the environmental crisis. In 'Anima Mundi: The Return of the Soul to the World',[22] Hillman puts a rather forceful challenge to all schools of psychoanalysis, arguing that if therapy neglects the soul of the world and concentrates only on the soul of the person, then it is merely contributing to the sum total of neurosis in the world. Hillman's attack on his own therapeutic tradition is put even more dramatically in his book *We've Had a Hundred Years of Psychotherapy and the World's Getting Worse*.[23] Although Hillman sometimes places himself on the side of the larger, 'ecological' soul and Jung on the side of the individual, narrowly human soul, it is clear to many of us within this tradition that Hillman is simply extending Jung's own original insights into the objective and cosmological dimensions of the soul. Hillman refers to the soul of the world as 'anima mundi', and in so doing he places his own research, and the Jung tradition generally, in league with neoplatonic philosophy and with the Florentine Renaissance.[24]

Hillman argues that 'man [humanity] exists in the midst of psyche; it is not the other way around. Therefore, soul is not confined by man, and there is much of psyche that extends beyond the nature of man'. He claims that all things in the world have mythopoetic dimension. Although soul is associated with 'innerness', it is wrong to claim this innerness for human persons; 'interiority is a metaphor for the soul's nonvisible and nonliteral inherence',[25] which is found everywhere, whether in animate or in so-called inanimate things. In a sense, Hillman extraverts our sense of interiority, so that it becomes a property of the world, just as he extraverts the notion of anima (in Jungian terms, the soul in man), so that it becomes the *anima mundi*, or soul of the world. Hillman's work has been very influential, and has given rise to a school of discourse on the *anima mundi*, a discourse based mainly in philosophy, phenomenology, and philosophical psychology.[26]

'Soul' as middle term between spirit and matter

James Hillman would argue that because we participate in a living cosmos, and because our human souls are linked to the world-soul or *anima mundi*, it is hardly surprising that we should feel ourselves to be influenced by the soul's presence or inherence in nature. This school of thought insists that we do not need an archaic theory about spirits in the land to account for our being influenced by landscapes or scenes, nor do we require a theory of anthropomorphic projection of human subjectivity into the outside world.[27] If we arrive at the view that we and the physical universe are enwrapped and enmeshed in a world-soul (a view which approximates to that of theoretical physics), then the flow and movement of emotional content and imaginal images between ourselves and the world is a logical consequence of being alive and in the world. Only a spiritually barren society would need to invent intellectual theories about the secret transmission of psychical life from subject to object.

A major advantage of the *anima mundi* concept over the spiritistic model is that it is open-ended, processual, and non-literal. Landscapes, countries, places do not 'have' or 'possess' spirits, but *are* phenomenological expressions of the world-soul. Different places express different states or conditions of soul. And importantly, the psychic dimension in nature would not impact upon all people in the same way. The influence of a place—or the *anima loci*—would differ according to the state of the human soul that is turned toward it. There would be a commingling or confluence of person and land in the psychic depths, and this could be envisaged as an alchemical interconnection, leading to any number of permutations and changes. The spirit-based model of land and earth would be far more constricting and mechanical: one or more fixed spirits in a place, or *genius loci*, would rise up from the land like ghosts or banshees, taking hold of their human subjects in predictable and predetermined ways. There would be hardly any room in this model for variation and difference, and no accounting for why different people experience landscapes and countries in contradictory ways. *Anima mundi* breaks the literalism and the monocentrism of the spiritistic model, and leads us forward toward postmodern complexity and diversity, rather than backward into premodern determinism and concretism.

What this imaginal vision means for the Australian psyche is far-reaching indeed. It points to the possibility of finding a middle way between Western mechanistic perception and Aboriginal metaphysical perception. That it should be the *soul* that offers this middle position is entirely appropriate and a time-honoured solution to an archetypal dilemma. In Renaissance cosmology, the soul or psyche was the middle term between spirit and matter: psyche is not heavy and inert like the concept of matter, nor transcendental and remote like spirit. Rather, psyche inhabits a middle area known as the *metaxy*, and is represented as subtle, elusive, imagistic and metaphorical. The soul and its imaginal world may be our way out of the crippling national dilemma between a Western materialism we are now tired of and an Aboriginal metaphysics we cannot readily access or fully embrace. The Euro-Australian temperament would not permit a shift toward a full-blown metaphysical or spiritistic order anyway, regardless of the political and cultural obstacles that bar that way (as discussed previously). An imaginal or metaphorical consciousness would give Australian society the numinous dimension that it so obviously lacks and needs. We can at least aspire to an imagination of place, allowing our psyche and the world-psyche space to move, freedom to be, and room to imagine. And Australia is infinitely imagine-able.

Australia becomes an ideal place for the birth of a new dreaming, a dreaming that could be an important cultural

experiment for the world at large. The thesis of white
rationality is being eroded by the antithesis of black
Dreaming, but the *synthesis* will probably combine and
transcend both terms in this cultural encounter. My own
experience in central Australia bore witness to the erosion
and destructuring of white rationality, but I did not feel that
this would simply be replaced by the indigenous antithesis.[28]
I always had a distant fascination for the bush hippies or so-
called white Aboriginals who would take on the indigenous
Dreaming as their own. As a young adult I enjoyed some of
their *ad hoc* rituals, even if at times they looked like
parodies of actual corroborees. But for me at least there was
something else to do, a different way to follow. The
synthesis of white rationality and black animism becomes, I
believe, a kind of postmodern animism, very close to the
vision that James Hillman is articulating. If we take the
mystical element from animism and the intellectual element
from rationality, we end up with a discerning or watchful
mysticism, a mysticism always on the alert for implausible
claims (a healthy capacity to detect nonsense), yet always
open to wonder and revelation. It may seem ironic that I
should have arrived at a theoretical understanding of a
possible Australian synthesis while studying with Hillman
in the United States. But these issues are, after all,
archetypal and universal, even if we must discover regional
solutions and responses to them.

Art before psychology: expressions of the new imagining

When I came back to Australia in 1984 I began searching
our literature for examples of imaginal vision, for
expressions of a dynamic relatedness to the land that could
provide a new basis for creative and transformative living. I
was heartened to discover that there was indeed a greal deal
of literary evidence to suggest that a new spiritual pact or

bond with landscape was developing here. Both Freud and Jung noted that every 'new' idea in psychoanalysis had been anticipated often well in advance by creative writers and artists. Nothing that Jung or Hillman might come up with about the (re)animation of nature or the objectivity of the soul would necessarily appear novel or new to Australian writers.

In fiction, Grant Watson stands out as an exponent of precisely the kind of new spirituality that I have in mind. If it were not for Dorothy Green's attentive scholarship and persistence, Watson might have completely disappeared from our cultural awareness. Obviously, there is a great deal of spiritual experience of the land in Patrick White, especially in *The Tree of Man* and *Voss*, where White makes deliberate connections between Euro-Australian 'mystical' experience of nature and the mythopoetic perceptual mode of the Aboriginal Dreaming. I have already written a book on White and I will resist the temptation to discuss him further here. There are also significant examples of a new mythopoetic response to landscape in the works of Martin Boyd, Katherine Prichard, Randolph Stow, and David Malouf. In recent fiction, Gerald Murnane comes closest to positing 'imagination' as a 'way', or imaginal vision as a mode of being in the world.

In popular culture, Michael Leunig's contribution to *anima mundi* or soul in the world has been outstanding.[29] For countless Australians, Leunig has disrupted the conventional envelope of the self, and allowed us to wander in a 'third dimension' of the soul—a world that is neither merely material nor elevatedly spiritual. In a secular society, which has reduced the popular artist–cartoonist to a satirical or 'funny' commentator on the political events of the day, Leunig has almost single-handedly won back for popular culture the different and more subtle reality of the soul. Leunig is the classic (re)discoverer of the 'inner' side of the 'outer' world; for him, as for Hillman, soul is not a private, subjective inwardness, but a public internal reality. Leunig has helped us to the realisation that psyche is not an entity that is confined to the church or clinic, but a dimension of human experience in which we all can share.

Imaginal vision is the stuff of poetry, it is the act by which things take on meaning and so become symbols and metaphors. Poetry itself is the major cultural carrier of the mythopoetic mode of perception in secular times. It is therefore not surprising to find that the best Australian poetry aspires toward the condition of mythopoesis, and that in this poetry an imaginal integration of the perceiving subject (the poet) and perceived object (the landscape) takes place. This kind of integration can be found in the most successful poems of Christopher Brennan, David Campbell, Francis Webb, John Shaw Neilson, Judith Wright, and Les Murray. But our so-called 'landscape poets' do not merely describe or represent the land, they *participate* in it. In our greatest poems, the old and habitual dualism between self and other is undermined, and the 'normal' condition of alienation is subverted. When that habitual dualism has been fully subverted, then the condition of poetry has been achieved. Great poetry is simply the achievement of mythopoesis.

The subversive power of our nature poets, however, is often denied in the rote teaching of this literature in schools and universities. Students of Australian poetry are most often told that the poets are simply 'representing' the land, not that they are reaching for a spiritual fusion with the landscape—which thereafter becomes no longer an external 'landscape' but a field of dreaming. It is little wonder that the poets have become increasingly cynical toward academics and teachers, and that in the case of Les Murray and Judith Wright actual complaints have been made about the educational use of their creative work. When these arguments flare up, I always betray my own profession and take the side of the poets, because the educational ideas that rule in this country are far behind what our poets and prophets are actually doing. An education system that is based on secular values and concerns can never understand poetry or the spiritual mission of the poet. The radical, threatening, challenging dimension in poetry is lost when poetry is taught without reference to its mythopoetic power. We do not hear mention of Wright's or Murray's direct encounter with the soul of the world, nor do we hear of Shaw Neilson's experience of the cosmic interiority of nature.[30] Teachers and academics talk about Neilson's 'personification' of nature, or they describe how Wright and Murray employ 'pathetic fallacy' or 'anthropomorphism' to poetic effect. Until we learn to respect the reality of soul, and until we can grasp that the world itself has soulful interiority, our poets will always be misrepresented as eccentrics supplying pretty adornment or fancy dress to the 'actuality' of nature. The unexamined assumption, of course, is that nature itself is neutral, blank, empty—a basic premise that poets simply do not share.

Entering the dream of nature

Neilson's poem 'The Orange Tree' (1919) is virtually a parable about the crazy dialogue or mis-conversation that takes place between the conscious 'knowing' intellect and the spontaneous 'experiencing' imagination in this country. Neilson personifies this dialogue within himself and within us all as a dialogue between a rational adult male and an intuitive young girl. The poem is narrated from the perspective of the male rational consciousness, which is unable to understand or fathom what the young child actually experiences when she says she is able to 'see' the mystical interiority and hidden light of the natural world. The poem begins:

The young girl stood beside me. I
   Saw not what her young eyes could see:
—A light, she said, not of the sky
   Lives somewhere in the Orange Tree.[31]

As the poem develops the adult enquirer puts one rational explanation after another in order to account for or explain away the intuitive experience of the child. He thinks that she may have fallen in love with a young boy, and that she is projecting this new excitation or animation upon the natural world.

—Is it, I said, of east or west?
   The heartbeat of a luminous boy
Who with his faltering flute confessed
   Only the edges of his joy?

This line of enquiry fails to work, and so he attempts other, more maudlin, leads related to the possibility of unrequited love, or to a possible recent bereavement, which may have unsettled or unduly animated the girl. The wonderfully accurate element here on Neilson's part is that all probings and postulations from the adult male relate to the feeling-life of the human sphere. The narrator simply cannot understand how anyone could get worked up about a mere orange tree, or, in Hillman's language, he cannot imagine how nature could be so spiritually animated as to have any passional or emotive impact upon human apprehension. He is caught up in the bubble of Australian rationality and intellectualism, which denies imaginal depth and resonance to the world, and which sees soul as residing only in human subjectivity.

In this poem the girl struggles hard to describe what she is seeing, or hearing, or feeling. The difficulty about intuitive experience of soul-in-the-world is that it cannot simply be collapsed into any one category of the five senses. It is not a sensate experience in the normal sense, and hence the girl frequently changes the sense-category of her own descriptions. First her experience is described as a light, then as a call, then a 'step'. But, in strategies reminiscent of mystical traditions such as Zen, Sufism, and Gnosticism, even as she offers a sense-category for her experience she immediately qualifies and even nullifies the category that she offers:

—Listen! the young girl said. There calls
No voice, no music beats on me;
But it is almost sound: it falls
This evening on the Orange Tree.

She hears a call that is not a call, a voice that is not a voice, a sound that 'is almost sound'. She attempts to reveal the truth of her experience by proceeding by negation: every category offered must be negated, because otherwise the 'otherness' of her experience will be collapsed, and the rational man will merely be able to nod his head in simple recognition, and his world will not be challenged. Here we think of the sense of the Chinese saying that 'the Tao that can be told is not the true Tao'. Finally, as the man's relentless and convoluted enquiries become totally exhausting, the girl puts an end to the charade by telling him to shut up:

—Silence! the young girl said. Oh, why,
Why will you talk to weary me?
Plague me no longer now, for I
Am listening like the Orange Tree.

There is, in the end, no rational explanation for the soul's powerful inherence in the natural world. There can be no simple description of imaginal vision that will meet the intellect's or the sensing mind's requirements. The girl is right to silence the man's nonsense, and to reaffirm, in the last line, the *act* of imaginal participation in the life of nature. Imaginal vision can only be achieved when the human barriers that separate us from nature are overcome. It is not that we must listen *to* the orange tree, but *like* the orange tree. Hillman has argued that it is only when something divine awakens in us that we can respond to the divinity of the world. The mythical interiority of the world simply will not present itself to our senses until we have awakened our own interiority and attuned our imaginal depths to the depths of nature. This will involve not more adult learning but rather 'unlearning' the ways of rational perception and becoming again like a child, in the sense of being capable of immediate apprehension of the cosmos.

Neilson, Wright, Murray as a poetic tradition of re-enchantment

Our tradition of imaginal receptivity to place begins fully with John Shaw Neilson, whose reputation has been rising steadily over recent decades. Neilson is, arguably, our most intuitive listener to the voice of things, or in other words, our best poet. However, he is certainly not the last word in Australian mythopoesis. Imaginal vision gains momentum and true psychological sophistication in the hands of Judith Wright, and it achieves a certain muscular intensity and mystical power in the writings of Les Murray. In this brief survey, I have neither the time nor the space to consider the imaginal achievements of other poets, and I apologise for my omissions.

Judith Wright seeks a kind of heightened perception of the natural world through psychical participation in nature. Although Wright is described as a nature-poet, she does not strive merely to admire or emulate nature, but to become like nature, to enter the inner life of nature. Like Neilson, she imagines that children are better able to experience the organic connection of the human and the natural. In poems such as 'The Child', 'Child and Wattle Tree', and 'The World and the Child', the figure of the child not only unites human and nonhuman worlds but acts as a personification of the cosmos itself. 'Take me into your life' says the inspired child of Wright's poem, 'till my feet are cool in the earth / and my hair is long in the wind; / till I am a golden tree spinning the sunlight'.[32]

In her famous *Woman to Man* poems of 1949 Wright argues that an awakened sexuality is able to supply the missing emotional link between consciousness and the earth. Through a heightened experience of our own bodies, and in Wright's case of the procreative powers of the female body, we are able to overcome our typically modern alienation and to feel nature as a transformative force within our own lives. Through the intense sexualisation of consciousness, nature is no longer just 'out there' but is very much an immediate and intimate experience. In 'Woman to Child' the female narrator is able to declare to the child:

> ... though you dance in living light
> I am the earth, I am the root,
> I am the stem that fed the fruit,
> The link that joins you to the night.

Again the message is that mere thought or cerebration will not carry us over the yawning gulf that separates us from nature, but only immediate emotional experience can quicken the archetypal life in us that spontaneously unites us again with our primal origin and source.

Imaginal vision in Australia means undoing all the old, safe clichés about 'the bush' and encountering the land anew as mysterious, numinous, and full of unknown voices. In 'Northern River' Wright discovers a gentle, receptive wisdom in the land: 'the river speaks in the silence / and my heart will also be quiet'. Wright finds poetry in every native tree, and at times she listens to 'the language of leaves', which is one of the indigenous languages of the continent. For Les Murray, landscape is a text full of inscriptions, parchments and archaic scribblings ('Dead Lagoon Scrolls') which need to be read by us, or by the imaginal eye within us. Unfortunately, the very act of concentrating on 'the bush' at all has, for some inattentive readers, turned Murray himself into a 'bushy' or bush cliché, so that he is seen to be perpetuating the old forms of experience that he is in fact challenging. A certain lack of concern for Murray's resacralising project has resulted in a lack of appreciation for the radical aspect of his work. Murray has been angered by this lack of respect for his work, but 'persistence in folly' (William Blake) is what is required: strength and vision must be found from the resacralising vision itself, not from the community of doubters and scorners.

Murray's 'Noonday Axeman' [33] is a Euro-Australian creation myth, a poem that traces with deft insight the history of white Australian responses to the land. In the early days of white settlement, Murray argues, it was necessary to build up barriers and defences against the land, to take away its primordial enchantment and to bolster our human resolve in the face of the vast and potentially disintegrative silences. His own forbears, the early axemen who still spoke in a Scots accent, spent a hundred years 'clearing, splitting, sawing' for the sake of creating 'a human breach in the silence'.

> A hundred years of timbermen, ringbarkers, fencers
> and women in kitchens, stoking loud iron stoves
> year in, year out, and singing old songs to their children
> have made this silence human and familiar.

Murray sees that it is at first necessary for an immigrant culture to impose its old songs and old stories upon the new land: 'men must have legends, else they will die of strangeness'. Murray indicates that those who failed to build a cultural defence or personal barricade against the Australian unknown were in danger of insanity and mental disintegration. This is a theme he might have borrowed from that troubled bush realist, Henry Lawson, who was only too aware of the disintegrative and dangerous aspects of the spirit of place. There were some, writes Murray, 'who fled to the cities, maddened by this stillness'. This primordial stillness, however, is still present in the land today. Upon experiencing this same stillness in what is only apparently 'the twentieth century', Murray is able to write:

And then, I know, of the knowledge that led my
    forebears
to drink and black rage and wordlessness, there will
    be silence.

While so clearly sympathetic to the problems of early colonial experience, Murray's crucial disclosure is that we no longer have to protect ourselves in the old manner. Murray believes that we must now embrace the land in a new way. We must learn to 'live in the presence of silence'. The old heroic manner of pitting oneself against the natural world will have to give way to a new receptivity and openness to the mystery of place. This will involve both a certain negative capability or humility on the part of the ego-personality, as well as a readiness to accept mystery and revelation from the land:

After the tree falls, there will reign the same silence
as stuns and spurs us, enraptures and defeats us,
as seems to some a challenge, and seems to others
to be waiting here for something beyond imagining.

Murray has grasped one of the central paradoxes of Australian experience: that what seems a defeat for the ego is also a liberation and release for the soul. The otherness of the land both 'enraptures and defeats us', it both 'stuns and spurs us': our rationality is stunned, but our yearning for contact with the soul of the world is spurred onward.

Suddenly, after two centuries of huddling and defensiveness, we stand in the presence of great mystery, and witness the enigma of a land that seems to be 'waiting here for something beyond imagining'. The Australian landscape inspires millennial or even apocalyptic fantasies. The vastness of the place and the hopelessness of the ego's desire to humanise, subdue, or tame the land, forces us to be mindful of the reality, power, and intentions of the nonhuman. No wonder the indigenous inhabitants lived in a state of perpetual mysticism, and by such poetic lines as 'Axe-fall, echo and silence. Dreaming silence', Murray subtly indicates that we too will become ensconced in a similar 'dreaming' based on our experience of the land. That this dreaming will always involve robust commitment, physical discomfort and egoic sacrifice is strongly indicated in this poem. An Australian spirituality can never become a sentimental or pallid thing, but will always remain existential, experiential, testing:

Axe-fall, echo and silence. Unhuman silence.
A stone cracks in the heat. Through the still twigs,
   radiance
stings at my eyes.

Rodney Hall: old, new, black and white dreamings

I hope to show you something less simple about the
country we are in, something outside the categories
you know ... I plan to stand by and wait until this
land, which is so near you and so unseen, enters your
heart too.
— *THE SECOND BRIDEGROOM*[34]

To close this brief survey of Australian re-enchantment I want to look closely at a contemporary novel. Rodney Hall has long been concerned, in his poetry and fiction, with the mythopoetic reawakening of consciousness. Hall wants us to discover a new dreaming, to re-enter the dream of nature, not by stealing the Dreaming from the Aboriginal people, but rather by drawing on the unconscious sources of creativity within the psyche itself. Rodney Hall has an abiding interest in what has virtually become a taboo topic in Australia: the transformative impact of Aboriginal Dreaming on the white psyche. He has nothing occult or metaphysical in mind, but, like me, he tends to feel that Aboriginal animism has a psychological impact on Euro-Australians, by first serving to erode the hardened layers of rationality, which may then give rise to a spontaneous spiritual transformation from within. The very presence of mythopoetic dynamics in Aboriginals could stir to activity the latent and repressed archetypal layers of the Euro-Australian psyche.

The central character of Rodney Hall's *The Second Bridegroom* is an escaped convict, a forger from the Isle of Man, who jumps ship off the coast of New South Wales in 1838, and flees inland to escape the authorities. After many long months in the forests, the convict finds himself momentarily trapped in a storehouse that contains grog and stationery. He resists the alcohol, picks up the stationery, and writes. The story has the benefit of hindsight, and the whole text, we discover, is a long love-letter written by the convict to the wife of the 'Master' to whom he is officially assigned as a labourer.

It is significant that the spontaneous (re)mythologising that is the subject of this book occurs after the loss or sacrifice of the convict's rationality. Culture-shock would understate what he experiences as he plunges into the wild and unfamiliar landscape. Reality falls apart as all the conventional signs that constitute the social fabric are left behind. 'I had arrived at a place where all my knowledge was useless' (p. 37). He enters a world of terrifying strangeness, where he has no names to fit what he sees and touches, and where some things are so unfamiliar that he fails to notice them at all. At first, his mind automatically struggles to impose a familiar order: 'My brain ... began to tackle the task of carving the chaos into bite sized meanings' (p. 13). However, he soon realises how futile this intellectual undertaking is, and he gradually attempts to allow the new-old land to speak for itself. 'When I could, I made a beginning: I promised not to try reading the messages I heard and smelled and touched, tasted and saw. I would respect them as having no use' (p. 21).

As he struggles to place himself in a new reality we see that, ironically, he has already been absorbed into the 'story' of another culture. He finds himself the central object of attention in an Aboriginal ceremonial journey. At first he does not even notice the silent, still, painted, and feathered men who have surrounded him. It becomes apparent to the reader, but evidently not to the protagonist, that these men are engaged in a ritual Dreaming walkabout, that they are moving from site to site in a bid to follow the songlines and renew the spirit of an ancient ancestor-being. An unbroken human circle is maintained throughout this ritual, and as the white man is discovered he is placed at the centre of the circle and becomes for the tribesmen a living incarnation of the spirit-being whom they have called up by their dancing and singing. Handled by a less skilled writer, this sequence could become problematical, perhaps even farcical. Hall allows a certain wry humour to emerge, but the humour is always contained and is never allowed to cut across either the sacredness of the Aboriginal performance nor the bewildered disorientation of the escaped convict.

The astonishing point about this sequence is that the convict's unaware participation in the ceremonial journey works to positive ends. From the Aboriginal point of view, the presence of this being from another world intensifies the Dreaming rituals, and provides a pivot at the centre of the magic circle. And not only is the convict himself kept physically alive and nurtured by this activity, but he also undergoes a profound spiritual transformation as a direct result of it. For his 'participation' in the Dreaming cycle results in an unexpected activation of his own mythic world. The intense exposure to Aboriginal sacred space has led to the awakening of sacred space within his own psyche. Yeats might say that his *spiritus mundi*, or World Memory, has been aroused; Jung would perhaps argue that the collective or familial unconscious has been activated. Hillman and Corbin would refer to the awakening of the *mundus imaginalis*, which in this case is shaped and conditioned by the myths of his cultural origin.

Although this man in his twenties is not consciously religious, we find that he becomes suddenly enmeshed in the Celtic mythology and folklore of his Isle of Man ancestry. He 'remembers' Celtic folksongs, myths, stories, and fairytales. He is also made to recall powerful childhood dreams in which pronounced mythic or archetypal motifs appeared. The Aboriginal emphasis on the bird-totem awakens in him imagery associated with Yllerion, the Celtic bird of fire. 'Here in New South Wales ... the real and the fabulous have not gone their separate ways. There is nothing to prevent our fables taking root here' (p. 17).

The convict from the Isle of Man has had a Christian upbringing, but this proves to be a fairly superficial layer of his mind which is overturned by the activation of a deeper, Celtic, pre-Christian layer. One myth in particular takes possession of him. It is the myth of the Celtic Goddess of Kirk Braddon and her doomed husband-lovers. Each year the Goddess took two bridegrooms, one for the winter, one for summer. 'Each had the task of killing the husband who had lain with her for the six months before him' (p. 65). The young man, dazed and overwhelmed by his encounter with mythic reality, is somehow co-ordinated by this myth, and increasingly comes to imagine himself the 'second bridegroom' of his Master's wife. He engages in mental and physical battles with the Master, who is subsequently slaughtered during an Aboriginal raid on the white settlement.

This is apparently an ancient myth that was destroyed when a summer-bridegroom refused to allow himself to be subjugated by the 'new winter king'. By refusing to submit to the matriarchal cycle, the doomed lover became a patriarchal king and so the old order was ruined: this prepared the way for patriarchal Christianity. But when this old order went down, there was a rumour that the myth could be revived if a second bridegroom appeared to renew the cycle. So, in a deranged and hallucinated state, in the pristine forests of the 'last foreign shore' and 'newest British colony', a runaway felon is engaged in the revival of an ancient Celtic mythologem. Where else to revive the primordial mythic psyche than in the most ancient and sacred continent on earth?

Rodney Hall has been seen by some commentators as foolhardy for taking up the sensitive topic of Aboriginal spirituality, but he shows a way that is clearly beyond white consumerist appropriations of Aboriginality. His theme is that living side-by-side with Aboriginality can set our own Dreamings going. Hall indicates that the politically responsible way for psychic renewal is the remythologising of *one's own* spiritual heritage. In the case of European-descended Australians, this means digging deep, deeper even than our Judeo-Christian tradition, which may be too dried out, too conscious or institutionalised, to foster spiritual renewal. Activating the indigenous archetype (Malidoma Some) may mean activating the lost or repressed 'indigenous' elements within the European traditions. But the challenge is to stimulate the mythic possibilities in one's own psyche, rather than to parasitically draw on others.

New dreaming and political awareness

> In Australian civilisation, I would contend, convergence
> between black and white is a fact, a subtle process,
> hard to discern often, and hard to produce evidence
> for. Just now, too, it lacks the force of fashion to drive
> it; the fashion is all for divisiveness now.
>
> — LES MURRAY[35]

'Political correctness' in contemporary society designates a good deal of what I have described above as out of bounds. But although political correctness is designed to support and protect the rights and values of indigenous minorities, I would argue that a fixed ideological position creates a cultural environment in which black and white reconciliation cannot take place. If a landscape-based spirituality is felt to belong only to the indigenous group, then we deny and exclude the very ground upon which responsible political action can take place. My belief is that only the mythopoetic renewal of Euro-Australia can lead to right political action insofar as the Aboriginal people are concerned. It is only by remythologising our Western psyche that we can begin to understand—and therefore to respect and appreciate—the mythologically-based Aboriginal psyche. Politicians and media commentators sometimes pay lip-service to the 'special relationship to the land' that is integral to Aboriginal culture, but unless non-Aboriginals have experienced a psychic connection to landscape they will not learn to respect the mythopoetic bond between this land and its indigenous inhabitants. Political goodwill alone will do very little to bridge the gap between cultures.

The same is true of our ecological crisis: we can urge each other to 'care more' about the environment, but until we have revised our sense of identity to *include* the natural world our best intentions may be in vain. The cure for our ecologically disastrous abuse of the earth and for our culturally debilitating racism is the spiritual renewal of consciousness. Whoever believed that spirituality and politics could be so intimately related? The discovery and development of a new imaginal vision will create the healing middle ground between Western rationality and Aboriginal animism, between ego-centred awareness and the living ecological earth. The only 'place' where the black and white cultures can genuinely meet is not in Canberra, the Department of Aboriginal Affairs, or the law courts, but in the imaginal world. The living soul is that barely explored mythic place where the conflict of archetypal forces in Australian society can be resolved.

9

Tracking the sacred in secular society

What happens to the Gods or archetypal forces in a secular society such as modern Australia? Do they 'die', go underground, or become irrelevant? Are they, as rationalists like to imagine, 'relevant' only for those who wish to believe in them? This problem has occupied me for many years, especially since I emerged out of the 'false enlightenment' of the atheistic and rationalist phase of my early adulthood. It is clearly not the case that society becomes bland, colourless, and cultureless when the celestial lights are turned out. It is rather that society becomes a demonic parody of sacred reality when society no longer recognises the divine sources from which its own life springs.

The Gods can be denied and rejected, but they can never be extinguished. They merely go into the unconscious, where they become sources of real psychological and social disturbance. They are no longer recognised by theologians or clergy, but only by doctors, alienists, psychotherapists, and poets. They puff up and inflate human ambitions and desires, and they attach themselves to the ego without its ever knowing. When the soul is lost to the unconscious, without any cultural or religious assistance toward its transcendent goals, it secretly distorts and corrupts our human activities, investing them with sublime and grandiose expectations that can never be met or realised at the human or sociopolitical level.

As a student at university I was taught to 'demystify' and 'see through' the symbolic worlds of religious and symbolic culture. Under the influence of those great cultural materialists and destroyers of illusions, Marx and Freud, I learnt to find infantile wishes behind concepts of God and deity, escapism behind the religious impulse, and oedipal incest behind the desire for transcendental bliss. However, I have since come to think that we must work in reverse: we must today 'see through' the messes and mishaps of secular society, and look for the buried Gods or archetypes in them. Mircea Eliade puts the situation well when he writes that we must

> attempt a demystification in reverse: that is to say, we have to 'demystify' the apparently profane world ... in order to disclose [its] 'sacred' elements, although it is, of course, an ignored, camouflaged, or degraded 'sacred'.[1]

This is Jung's own strategy, but it is not clear from Eliade's work whether he arrived at this position independently or under Jung's influence. The task of contemporary wisdom, as Jung sees it, is not to discredit the religious symbolism of the past or to 'explode the myths' of a former time, but to locate, track down, and understand the contemporary vestiges and unconscious remnants of the sacred that persist even in our own secular or profane time.

Inhuman elements in human experience

> The spirit doesn't die, of course; it turns into a monster.
>
> — CHRISTOPHER KOCH[2]

We enter modern life with impossible dreams, expecting our partners, friends, and relatives to be God-like and infallible; or we place media celebrities and political personalities upon exalted altars, viewing them as a sort of pantheon of deities in a secular heaven. We expect this political programme or that human relationship to grant us paradise, utopia, or a glimpse of divine grace, and not surprisingly we frequently lapse into a slough of despond and depression, cursing life for failing us yet again. We are quite content to be unconsciously possessed by religious expectations and transcendental desires, but, perversely, we will not allow these expectations and desires a religious outlet or goal, but must always direct these desires toward the human and material level.

And so we seek all manner of vulgar substitutes for spiritual satisfaction. Drug addiction and the burgeoning drug epidemic in this and other countries is an unconscious and miscarried expression of the need to find ecstatic release from the prison-house of the alienated ego. Despite our intellectual dedication to rational and egotistical goals, we unconsciously crave an experience of the nonegoic and the transcendent, which is artificially but destructively reproduced in drugs. Similarly, the so-called sex revolution of our century is an unconscious expression of the archetypal desire to connect in ecstatic and releasing ways with an Other. In our secular world the Other has lost its capital 'O' dimension and has become an 'other' human being, a lover, a friend, a husband or wife; or, more often, *the other* man or woman in our lives, since it is the illicit affair that often carries more psychical and archetypal resonance than the partner to whom we are officially wedded. Connection with the other leads to forbidden and taboo sexual liaisons with the secretive other, to that which is not part of our conscious world. We see how easily the unconscious desire for the sacred becomes expressed as promiscuous sexuality or as an erotic and personal parody of the union of self with the divine.

With divine imperatives brought to bear upon sexuality

we find that it too sometimes collapses under the weight of expectations. People sometimes shift from promiscuity to frigidity or total abstinence because what they were seeking from sexuality could not be found. Or some people give up on the opposite sex and turn to same-sex love as a move toward self-regeneration and rebirth. Often the dreams of such persons will indicate that their erotic feeling must be moved from the human to the divine, and dreams may put forward powerful archetypal symbols in order to help transform psychic energy from the one level to the other. Dreams strive to come to our psychological assistance, but very often they are not heard or properly understood, especially if interpreted according to the sexual and reductive theories of mainstream psychoanalysis, whence their great attempts to create 'symbols of transformation' are tragically defeated by the materialist cast of mind that 'interprets' their meaning.

If sex and drugs do not attract us, or backfire when attempted, there is always the orgy of consumerism to consider. Emotionally we are empty, so we try to fill the emptiness with goods, objects, clothes, food, services, and, when these bore us, there are the big luxury items and highly expensive services, as well as trips to exotic places where we try for a glimpse of what lies beyond routine reality and the mundane ego. The consumer society is powerfully activated by the degraded sacred, even if all of it is carefully manipulated and controlled by our cool-headed entrepreneurial mind. The innate archetypal impulse is for *more*. The buried soul in us, which has become a blind autonomous impulse, knows there is more to reality than what we already have or know, and so we are compelled from within to seek more and more at the material level. It is not that material things are bad or that money is evil: this is the world-denying position of old-fashioned, pre-psychological and puritanical religion. It is rather that material things, money, drugs, sex, relationships, are often *invested* with perversely inappropriate spiritual longings and inhuman archetypal expectations.

We arrive at the paradox that we profane and denigrate the material world when we are unconsciously bound to it by the compulsive projection of the spiritual. We overburden the physical by asking it to perform magical tricks and to produce miraculous satisfactions. Matter itself is a manifestation of the sacred, but when we cut ourselves off from the divine source, matter then becomes demonic. In traditional religious terms, the figure of Satan, who is nothing other than a *fallen* angel, a gross parody and distortion of the sacred, has got into our lives and controls our behaviour. Or again in traditional religious language (which we are unable to read symbolically any more): by denying God we unwittingly court the Devil. When the sacred falls into the unconscious it becomes demonic, generating all manner of psychosomatic symptoms, irrational compulsions and obsessions, and other mental disorders.

Where have the Gods got to in secular and enlightened times? Jung replies that 'the Gods have become diseases';[3] having fallen from heaven, the Gods now reappear in our own unconscious with a terrible vengeance. The transcendent powers thrash around in our psyches and bodies, causing neurosis and forcing us toward bizarre literal enactments of symbolic processes. Secretly the repressed Gods pursue their patterns and interests in and through our lives, bringing morbidity and distortion to the human world. Ultimately, this activity makes a mockery of the supposed freedom of the ego-personality. Popular culture, cinema, science fiction, and other aesthetic expressions of postmodern society are teeming with images and narratives that indicate that despite what we think, our secular society and our rational minds are completely co-ordinated, and indeed possessed, by archetypal contents and figures. In countless novels and movies, the 'other' presents itself as something alien, archaic, weird, and yet that other insists on making its presence felt and in running rampant through the safe precincts of our narrowly human world. The power of the alien intruders is all the more awesome and autonomous because we fail to understand our relationship to them; we ironically give the Gods or demons more sway over us by disowning them.

The modern denial and the search for freedom

In ancient times, our condition would readily be recognised as one of *hubris*, arrogance, or inflation. When humanity forgets or wilfully denies the Gods, when it thinks it is itself God, able to live and be without the Gods, then it succumbs to hubris and perforce must deal with the punishment and vengeance of the Gods. Hubris was the most feared moral transgression in the ancient world, and much Greek tragedy arose from the need to give it public and aesthetic expression. Tragic heroes are those who strive too hard, overstep human boundaries, outreach their own and human limits, and so instigate their own downfall as they bring upon themselves the terrible punishment of the Gods. What was viewed once as divine vengeance and wrath can be seen today as archetypal possession and psychic upheaval— rather than literal Gods or holy fires attacking us from above, we can now see that nonhuman agents in the psyche are wreaking devastation and havoc.

Although the classics are full of warnings and signals about this condition, and ways to handle or avoid it, we do not benefit from this cultural wisdom because we fail to appreciate how any of it relates to us today. For us, our condition is not classical hubris but 'intellectual enlightenment'. We see ourselves as free-wheeling, unattached, unbounded, rather than as unconsciously possessed and enslaved by archetypal forces. We mistake the *mania* and *fury* of the Gods for our own high energy and soaring libido. We also have our own strictly rational, secular terms and understandings for the madness that has befallen us: anxiety, stress, neurosis, the tension and pace of modern life. But when the manic forces of the Gods have run their course, they simply dump us into a pit of depression, where we are suddenly made aware of how little personal energy and human resources we actually possess. Even then, we say: oh, that's just life, the ups and the downs.

Our greatest spiritual fault is not even guessing that an Other might be involved in what we are pleased to call our manic-depressive cycles. We see that we suffer from real ailments, but these are felt to be the logical cost of living in a fast world. We still maintain the old positivist belief that our neurotic problems and manic cycles will eventually be overcome by science and medicine as we make our way toward a paradise of complete knowing. But our very paradigm of knowing is deficient, because it does not admit the wisdom that has to do with ultimate reality, with the correct relationship between the human and the sacred.

In Australian writing, a remarkable expression of what I am describing can be found in Patrick White's great novel *The Solid Mandala* (1966):

> After he retired, Dad would sometimes recall, in the spasmodic phrasing which came with the asthma, his escape by way of Intellectual Enlightenment, and the voyage to Australia, from what had threatened to become a permanence in black and brown, but in the telling, he would grow darker rather than enlightened, his breathing thicker, clogged with the recurring suspicion that he might be chained still.[4]

The 'intellectual enlightenment' and the journey to Australia are significantly connected in this passage: both are seen as escapes from the encumbrances of the past, ways of transcending the religious mentality and burdensome tradition. And yet 'in the telling' of this tale of apparent escape and freedom the teller 'grows darker rather than enlightened, his breathing thicker, clogged with the recurring suspicion that he might be chained still'. The rationalist denial of the sacred simply gives rise to a darker, more morbid and morose, form of bondage, because it is an *unconscious* and unknowing bondage to archetypal forces. This unconscious bondage is detrimental to the ego's health and is life-threatening, as is evident in this miraculous one-sentence description of the plight of George Brown; he is freed from the Old Country, yet dumbly suffering from spiritual malaise. Mircea Eliade could have been speaking about the George Browns of this world when he wrote: 'Modern nonreligious man forms himself by a series of denials and refusals, but he continues to be haunted by the realities that he has refused and denied'. [5]

The history of modernity and of the last few hundred years is the history of the ego's struggle for absolute autonomy and freedom. The rise of humanism in the Renaissance, and later in the eighteenth century Enlightenment, is the rise of the ego's desire to be rid of the past and its superstitions. Humanism, science, and the intellect conspired to create a secular world in which man was the measure of all things, in which matter and the laws of the universe were rationally explicable, and in which humanity was master over creation. The dream of the Enlightenment was a dream of liberty and freedom, which began to express itself in political and cultural revolutions, in radical changes to social and moral values, and in the new sciences and arts. Many great and liberating achievements were made, not least of which was the impassioned opposition to tyranny in Church and State, in secular institutions and in the workplace. Humanism has performed many social and political miracles, and we are all 'better off' because of it.

But we are not any *better* because of it. Despite its political and social achievements, humanism has left us culturally impoverished and spiritually bankrupt.[6] God is dead, moral and spiritual values have been declared entirely relative and arbitrarily constructed, the soul and spirit find no solace or nourishment, communal ties and traditional bonds are weakening and falling apart, narcissistic individualism is rampant, and Western civilisation finds itself sliding inexorably into degradation. The Gods have certainly wreaked havoc on us, and most likely will continue to do so until humanity forges a new pact with them. The dreadful irony is that humanism began as a development to win us absolute freedom, liberty, and an earthly paradise. Instead, we have simply become enslaved to the ego, to the lower instincts, and to all the unconscious archetypal forces that course through us and take easy possession of us.

The great religions have long taught that the ego cannot be its own master and cannot achieve absolute freedom. If it attempts to reach beyond its limits, it rapidly degenerates and loses its integrity. As the popular saying has it, the ego makes a good servant but a lousy master. The ego's task in the psyche, like humanity's task in creation, is to serve a greater reality (Jung), to attend to the needs of an Other (Eliade), to further the incarnation in this world of unmanifest Being (Heidegger). The ego can either *choose* a life of service or *be made to serve* in various involuntary and destructive ways. The choice is between a relative freedom or no freedom at all. No other option seems available to us. There is 'freedom' only in the ego's conscious decision to choose what it must do. This is the central paradox of many religions, as it is of archetypal psychology: *only by entering into deliberate service can the individual become free.* In my commitment to servitude is my happiness; in my acceptance of bondage to the divine is my liberty. The modern individual, paradoxically speaking, only achieves a degree of freedom when he or she renounces the illusion of complete independence, and accepts, along with ancient and premodern humanity, that he or she exists in relationship with an Other who must be propitiated, served, and recognised. I agree with Camille Paglia when she says that the contemporary emphasis upon freedom is misconceived and delusive, and that 'freedom is the most overrated modern idea'.[7] Absolute freedom is the construction of a power-oriented ego that believes it can rule alone in the house of personality and in the outside world.

In archetypal terms, secular humanism is the product of the hubristic ego, whose course or pattern is determined in Western society by the patriarchal hero. The hero is an important and much-needed denizen of the psyche and the masculine principle he embodies is crucial in the scheme of things, but he and his masculinity tend to overwhelm other figures and presences in the soul, and the hero has a habit of becoming dictatorial and oppressive. His main project is the promotion of himself and the eradication of the opposition. *His* idea of freedom is what we are all suffering from today, and what now threatens the stability and structure of Western civilisation. 'Freedom' for the ego is licence, the ability to do what it likes, the freedom to run rampant in the psyche and in the world without any regard for the Other. In many hero-myths, not only in ancient Greece but also in other mythological cosmologies, the hero has to be stopped either by men, women, or the Gods, lest he bring total devastation. In the Hero Cycles of the Winnebago Indians, the Twins become inflated by their own powers, and when their power-lust causes them to kill one of the four animals that holds up the earth, they are soon arrested and slain. As Joseph Henderson writes, 'The hero's symbolic death becomes a sign that a new level of psychic maturity has been achieved'.[8]

Cultural development through the archetypal feminine

In contemporary Western societies, feminism, ecology, eco-feminism, and numerous other social liberationist movements are attempting to bring about the patriarchal hero's symbolic death, and thus to establish the new level of psychic maturity of which Henderson speaks. Ecology and feminism are charged archetypally with the mission of arresting the runaway heroic ego, and with tripping up the schoolboy philosophy of unlimited expansion and development. Today, in Australia, the new cry is for sustainable development, and virtually every educated person looks with some disdain at social, economic, political, and personal displays of hegemonic masculinity and patriarchal excess. The patriarch, the hero, and the archetypal masculine are in widespread disrepute, and must be brought down. This cultural revolution involves political and social action, but it must be understood that the masculine and patriarchy are archetypal principles of the human psyche, and that our liberation from these elements must be conducted at psychological and spiritual levels, as well as at sociopolitical ones. If a social revolution is to be effective, it must take place simultaneously in inner and outer theatres. To liberate the soul from the over-reaching and destroying hero, a depth psychological transformation is required within the human psyche.[9] Feminism and ecology can only be agents for change at this deeper, spiritual level if they genuinely mythologise themselves and become alert to the numinous archetypal forces upon which they are based and from which they gain their power in the first place.

In numerous myths, the hero must be checked or

compensated by the *anima*, soul, or feminine dimension of the psyche. The anima represents the principle of eros, the drive toward unity, whereas the hero personifies logos, the urge toward separation. The hero's credo is 'divide and conquer', whereas that of the soul is 'only connect'. The soul has a very different conception of freedom and a different understanding of self-fulfilment to that of the ego. The soul finds its freedom through relationship and relatedness, through reaching out to what is beyond itself. The soul's liberation, caught as it is initially within the confines of the personal self, is to reach out beyond the human to the transcendent sacred, to connect its own reality with the greater reality of the *anima mundi*, the soul of the world. The anima or soul knows well that only by connecting with something greater can liberation be achieved. As yet, in Australia, we do not have models for this important process of spiritual liberation: we have models and images about how to identify with the rational ego, but when it comes to breaking out of that prison we only have negative or inferior images such as dropping out, getting drunk, taking drugs, nervous breakdown. What we urgently lack are cultural, positive, religious models for the transcendence of the ego, and until these models are found Australian society will be plagued by negative or inferior expressions of the longing to step outside the rational ego that imprisons us.

The myths indicate that the soul is actively constellated when the hero has outlived his usefulness, or when his unchecked power threatens the survival of the world. At that moment, eros values begin to replace logos values, relatedness eclipses conflict, and *knowing with an other* (the true meaning of the word 'consciousness')[10] replaces egotistical and divisive knowing for its own sake. In important ways, our society is already moving in this direction, although to a large extent the revolution has been caught up in the sociopolitical dimension and has not been allowed to become the deeper spiritual and psychocultural change that it must become. It is perhaps inevitable that in a thoroughly secularised society, the very forces that would free us from our humanistic prison are themselves secularised. The archetypal feminine wells up from the collective unconscious and feminism is born. But unless the Goddess herself is allowed to be born out of the sea-spray and foam created by the severed genitals of the old patriarch, we have missed the mythic opportunity of the time. So too, archetypal eros wells up from the depths and suddenly ecological awareness and the 'Gaia' hypothesis are born. But unless ecology is allowed to carry this eros and the romantic splendour of the unified cosmos we have not fully obeyed the dictates of the compensatory *Zeitgeist* or spirit of the time.

Beyond God the Father[11]

'God is dead, anyway—thank God—in Australia.'[12] Only Nietzsche, the foolhardy, and some Australians would be perverse enough to find relief and delight in what is the great metaphysical catastrophe of the modern era. But it is apparent that the old patriarchal dominants have gone into decline, that God the Father has waned or is 'dead', and everything that was built up around the *senex* or father archetype will suffer destabilisation and be made to appear relative and problematical. 'Things fall apart; the centre cannot hold', Yeats wrote in 'The Second Coming', intuiting that the two-thousand-year cycle of Christianity was about to end, to be replaced by a system antithetical to it. 'What rough beast', Yeats asks, 'its hour come round at last, / Slouches towards Bethlehem to be born?'[13] Depth psychology would reply that the rough beast is the primordial unconscious itself, stirred to activity by the collapse of the old patriarchal order, and currently being 'born' into society and consciousness. The rising archetype, according to Yeats, was the sphinx, a figure emerging from the *Spiritus Mundi* or world memory of humankind, with a 'lion body' and 'the head of a man'. The intuitive Yeats hardly needed Jung's theory of archetypal compensation, since he had arrived at the same idea himself, in poetic, not psychological, language: 'Our civilization was about to reverse itself or some new civilization about to be born from all that our age had rejected'.[14]

Mythologically, the sphinx is a feminine-matriarchal figure, with ancient associations with goddesses, death and rebirth, and the chthonic earth. It is an image of the dark, primordial, and unmanageable Other. The sphinx is what arises in Yeats's 'world memory' after the collapse of patriarchy, the Church, and God the Father. Some people read 'The Second Coming' as a prophecy of doom, a sign that we are headed for a chaotic future, which will be ruled over by a loathsome beast and the Anti-Christ. However, this seems to me to be a rather dismal and literal reading. When the unconscious is first released, either in the collective or the individual psyche, it frequently presents itself to consciousness as something shocking and formidable. After shrinking with fear from the image of the sphinx, we may be able to see that it is, after all, imaginal and psychic; part beast, part human. Everything psychic is capable of transformation, and the sphinx is no exception, since it brings with it, or symbolises, the teeming life of the imaginal realm. It is full of psychological energies, pagan forces, earthly libido. Only a puritanical consciousness constructs the sphinx as the Anti-Christ, as the devil, as satanic. A mature consciousness sees through the 'satanic' appearance to the enormous reservoir of raw, instinctual energy that the sphinx contains. We have to dispense with the rigidly defended ego, which sets up the unconscious as loathsome or despised Other, and allow the sphinx to be born in a holy place, to present itself to our consciousness as significant archetypal Other.

This sphinx slouches towards Bethelehem to be born. Historically, the divine reveals itself in the least expected places. In Christianity, the Most High reveals itself in the lowliest stable. I believe that in these post-industrial, post-rationalist, and post-patriarchal times the divine must inevitably reveal itself in and through the archetypal feminine, and through the animal and vegetable realms over which the Great Goddess has traditionally presided. The world of the feminine and of primordial nature already has the glow of myth and magic about it, as if a mythic breakthrough or revelation is at hand. Yeats will be proved right: all those forces that oppose or contradict Christianity and the Judeo-Christian world, especially the pagan deities of nature, sexuality, and matter, long repressed, and the feminine goddesses of life, the natural cycle, the earth, and instinct, long held in abeyance by the ruling *senex* tradition, will be released into consciousness, for good or ill. This will usher in a new paganism and a new polytheism,[15] as Yeats shrewdly observed. The key features of contemporary society are already clearly identifiable as expressions of the shadow side of Judeo-Christianity: plurality, diversity, the decline of patriarchy and masculine heroics, the release of sexuality, the destruction of time-honoured authorities and of numerous social and familial forms, and the radical relativisation of mores, values, and attitudes. The new spirituality will arise directly from these contemporary social phenomena, and will simply represent a dawning awareness of the awesome mythic power at the heart of what we are already experiencing at social and political levels.

The cultural pendulum is swinging in the opposite direction: the so-called 'new age' (which is really the return of a very old age) is a much underrated social force in

Australia, and is a matriarchal and goddess-based movement that represents a compensatory swing in the opposite direction to mainstream patriarchal society. Yeats said that 'because we had worshipped a single god (the new civilisation) would worship many'.[16] As the masculinist pubs, churches, convents, and barber shops go broke or close down in Australian cities, new age bookshops and 'awareness centres' are popping up everywhere, offering the public a broad range of largely non-Christian, non-patriarchal esoteric arts and sciences, such as astrology, tarot, I Ching, karma sutra, sacred sex, herbalism, naturopathy, meditation, yoga, psychic massage, channelling, neopaganism and wicca, martial arts, reincarnation, Eastern religions and philosophies, Native American vision quests and goddess spirituality. In this growing sub-culture, the values of eros, soul, and body are held in high esteem, whereas mind, intellect, logos are regarded with a good deal of suspicion. Buckminster Fuller's admonition that we 'lose our mind and come to our senses' encapsulates the ideology of the new age. The 'new age' is the social and political counterpart to the visionary sphinx, which arises at the moment patriarchy starts to decline. Like the sphinx, it is sensual, unfathomable, frightening: heralding the return of feminine mystery to the dried-out world of patriarchal society.

We stand today between two worlds: the old patriarchal order, and the 'new' eruption of ancient, non-establishment sciences and mysteries. The 'old' world is Euro-centric, and, for Australians, British, whereas the 'new' is Asian, Middle Eastern, and inspired by indigenous cultures throughout the world. The challenge for Australians is to attempt an integration of the two worlds: not to cling fearfully to the old, nor to throw out the old in favour of the new, but to find a new balance, a new point of cultural and personal equilibrium. In contemporary society, we have the excesses and tyranny of the patriarchal institutions on the one side, and the excesses and indulgences of the matriarchal counter-culture on the other side. It is left to the individual to negotiate his or her vital course between these extremes, since by definition 'individuation' means finding a new way and not becoming absorbed or identified with mass movements or collectivities. Finding a new way implies alienation, loneliness, and, above all, an acceptance of psychological conflict between the warring parts of the psychic totality. We can be sure that Australian society will see plenty of conflict in the future, as the values and attitudes of the archetypal feminine engage in an epic battle with the dominants of patriarchal culture. A great danger in Australian society, which is very literal-minded and not spiritually sophisticated (we really have no concept of 'universal forces' like Yin and Yang at work) is that 'masculine' and 'feminine' get rigidly attached to men and women, so that the battle of archetypal forces degenerates to a gender war. Journalists exploit this literalism for its sensational value, and very few voices can be heard arguing that the 'feminine' and the 'masculine' are symbolic principles inside all of us, demanding subtle, complex and difficult adjustments by men and women alike.

Postmodern chaos and 'negative capability'

In the so-called 'modern' era creative artists felt that they inhabited a spiritual wasteland, in which traditional religions had become 'a heap of broken images' (Eliot) and in which the human soul went unnourished and unattended. The modern individual suffered from a frightening sense of alienation and despair, and an awareness of a profound discontinuity from the past. This was the 'death of God' era, the era of Nietzsche, Eliot, Freud, Hardy, Yeats, and existentialism.

In the postmodern era we find ourselves in a vastly

different psychospiritual situation, with a new set of problems and challenges. The psyche, like nature, abhors a vacuum, and the vacuum left by the decline of the patriarchal dominants has invited into the soul a plethora of religious and archetypal images. This metaphysical 'inundation' has coincided with, and been furthered by, the enormous explosions and developments of modern technology, whose 'information highway' and commercial productions have made available virtually every religious tradition, cult, or cosmology known to human history. In society, countless numbers of symbolic and mythological systems are for sale in the new age supermarket, while inside, from the unconscious, we are also assailed by strange forms and alien images. Postmodern spirituality resembles Hiroshima after the bomb: new life grows from the wreckage of the old cultural order; strange new plants, mutants or exotic species of symbolic life push up from the rubble and move toward the sun.

These images are not the 'heap of broken images' of T.S. Eliot's 'The Waste Land', but are highly charged with psychic energy and religious meaning. It is because these new images are so persuasive, so full of mana, that so many new religious cults are springing up everywhere in the Western world. Cults are not arising because people are going crazy, or because the world is going down the drain and people are less intelligent than they were (a view with a surprising currency), but because aspects of the living spirit have invaded their hearts, and their lives are never the same again. We have got to *understand* the new religious phenomena, not merely criticise them from a position of intellectual superiority or patriarchal arrogance. While political feminism sweeps through the university, government, and major social institutions, a kind of 'spiritual feminism' sweeps through the streets and the wider community, promoting the arcane wisdom of the archetypal feminine, lost goddesses, and forgotten matriarchal arts and sciences. It is a great pity that the connection between these two kinds of feminism is not better known, and better respected, because until society as a whole becomes alert to the spiritual demands of the uprising feminine, we will continue to be bombarded with cults, ideologies, and eccentric 'movements'. What the official culture fails to see or integrate, the unofficial counter-culture will be forced to act out in often excessive and fanatical ways.

The problem today is not, as in the existential period, whether or not a sacred order exists. We live in a veritable sea of sacred images, religious longings, and metaphysical convictions. Our real problem is how to properly honour, recognise, and serve the new sacredness that has erupted. We are incoherent, confused, and illiterate before the divine, and we seriously lack a cosmology, a framework, a postmodern theology, to make sense of the sacred and its influence upon us. Unfortunately, the very word 'postmodern' has an academic ring to it, so that the insights that postmodern philosophy may have to offer are seen as exclusively academic, not available to the wider community. The university can tell the public why the 'modern' has ended and why the 'postmodern' has begun, but as yet it has failed to get this message across, and this is a direct result of academic exclusivity and jargon.

I believe that the major challenge today is to stay with the uncertainty, the chaos and confusion, and not to want or expect firm answers, complete systems, or clear models. We must attempt to explore our confusion, examine it, and not rush back to the past for a bygone order, nor move sideways to completely embrace (in often uncritical or romantic ways) the religious systems of other cultures. We have to learn to remain in the present with an attitude of what Keats called 'negative capability', which is the ability to be in doubts, uncertainties and mysteries without any irritable search after fact or reason. We live in 'interesting times' and the temptation is always to wish that things were otherwise, that life were simpler, more basic, with less tension. These times require a certain courage or openness, since we are forced to live on the wild side, to question and doubt so much, to walk over the rubble of the past while at the same time encountering the raw and unformed energies that will become the archetypal foundations of a future world-view. We owe it to the future to ensure that culture moves forward in an authentic manner, and that the 'solutions' discovered for our spiritual crisis are not spurious or false.

10 ▶

The transformation of spirit

This book has attempted to briefly sketch an archetypal process that is occurring in the Australian context and yet is of universal significance. This process is the age-old cycle of the death, disintegration, and eventual rebirth of the spirit. The proud, European, patriarchal, heroic spirit came to Australia to conquer yet another foreign land, to extend the empire of Britannia into a new quadrant of the globe. This colonising project succeeded to some extent, especially in material and social institutional terms. But, as Lawrence noted, the 'spirit' of Europe had disappeared, changed, or had been eclipsed by a different psychic reality. Spirit does not transport as readily as rum or mahogany. Many tried to feign the European spirit here: these were the progressive colonialists who were not in touch with the inside reality. Professionals of the Church and the spiritual world, who were mostly in league with the colonialist project, emphasised the universal mission of the Church and at first paid little attention to the sense of place or to the displacement of the old spirit.

A new breed developed in nineteeenth-century Australia who were generally antipathetic toward colonialists and the clergy. These were the so-called 'real Australians', and they were pragmatic, resourceful, down-to-earth, stoical, laconic, ironic, white, masculinist, and heavily defended against foreign elements both in the world and inside the psyche.

This breed lived aggressively at the surface of life. These men and women were existentialists without knowing it; fashionable ahead of their own time. They did not need Nietzsche to tell them God was dead, nor did they need Freud to announce that instinctuality was primary. Nor did they need Marx or Lenin to inform them that social redemption would come from the empowerment of the working class. The early white Australians were naturally egalitarian, instinctual, secular, and godless: they were modernists and existentialists on horseback. They were this way because, like Nietzsche, Freud and Marx, they had experienced the death of the spirit, which was the lynch-pin around which Western culture had been constructed, the central axis that made the establishment of Jewish-Christian high culture possible. When that axis was destroyed or attacked, the vast structures would tumble and fall, although in most Western societies this decline is being heroically resisted and delayed.

In the Western world, spirit has over-reached itself, gone too far too quickly, and has suffered exhaustion. The great modern intellectuals did not kill the spirit, but have merely diagnosed its terminal illness. Spirit surged wildly ahead, obsessed with fantasies of technological progress, rational enlightenment and limitless development. It wanted not only to change and improve on nature, but to leave nature and the archetypal feminine behind in its bid for perfection and rational order. Not surprisingly, nature has rebelled against this fascistic enterprise. The natural and instinctual forces, repressed or denied by spirit, have been erupting with catastrophic force throughout this century. Judeo-Christian civilisation has been ravaged by the forces of brute aggression, greed, desire, instinct—all the vices that Christian virtue felt it had overcome. Whole structures of the pre-Christian pagan world have been unearthed and realised in our time: Nietzsche incarnated in his own person the figure of Dionysus Zagreus, Freud rediscovered Oedipus and pagan sexuality, Jung incarnated the Trickster Hermes-Mercurius, Hitler enacted a demonic version of the Nordic Wotan, and numerous dictators and cult leaders have personified the Anti-Christ. Ours is certainly the age marked by the insignia of the beast, not because the beast is demonic, but because we have made the beast demonic by longing too much for sublime order.

The death of the spirit is a world-wide cultural phenomenon, which is hardly unique to Australia. In this book I have simply been sketching the regional enactment of this archetypal drama. The geographical location of Australia at the farthest edge of the known world gave dramatic representation to the motifs of descent, decline, and degeneration.[1] In Australia, European spirit met an archaic and powerful nature that was more than its equal. Our first poet of real importance, Charles Harpur, wrote: 'Lo, 'tis the Land of the grave of thy father!'[2] Australia became a site for the death of the hero, the father, and the patriarchal spirit. Chris Wallace-Crabbe wrote, 'Though much has died here, little has been born'.[3] Our greatest national figures and legends, Voss, Richard Mahony, Burke and Wills, Leichhardt; our greatest iconographic national sites, Uluru (Ayers Rock), Hanging Rock, Gallipoli, the Outback, are all places or figures of loss, sacrifice, and ruin.

With all this doom and gloom to report, one would imagine that we should all retreat into depression, hurt, and despair. But that is not at all the message that I am trying to impart in this book. The argument here is that the death of the old spirit is a cultural and psychological necessity. Nature is wild, rebellious, and a fearful opponent to any arrogant or haughty spirit that denies her. But my own belief, inspired by Jung, gnosticism, and mythopoetic tradition, is that nature is not a malign force bent on destroying us. Ultimately, nature is drawing the hubristic patriarchal spirit back into herself, not to destroy spirit but to *transform* it. The death of the old gives way to something new, and the new is yet to be born. 'It is the time for a new beginning, but not quite yet. First, the old must be buried, and with due rites.'[4] It is still too early to tell what is being prepared, but, as Beckett put it, 'something is taking its course'.[5]

As discussed in the previous chapter, the new revelation will be grounded in the feminine, but it may not necessarily *be* feminine. Spirit has been plucked from the skies and returned to the earth, not to be buried there, but to prepare for its own transformation. The new revelation may be based on a spirit that has been forced off its pedestal and brought into new, redemptive contact with the chthonic earth and the feminine. What we are experiencing, as yet without the aid of a messianic figure or a Second Christ, is the further incarnation of the divine. In the First Incarnation, God became man, but He did not wed the feminine. It was a partial incarnation, and the gnostic tradition realised as early as the second century AD that Christ's mission was not final and revelation was not complete.[6] Gnosticism has for centuries attempted to conceive and even bring about the so-called Third Age of the Spirit: after the era of the Father (Judaism) and of the Son (Christianity), comes the cosmic New Order or Third Realm, whose task will be to engage in a further and deeper incarnational relationship with creation.[7]

In the new revelation, which is profoundly ecological in character, the spirit cannot wander alone but is drawn into nature in order to enliven and divinise nature, while also transforming and incarnating itself. Rilke captured the yearnings of nature for a new transcendence in his famous ninth elegy:

Earth, is it not this you want: an invisible
Resurrection in us?—Is not this your dream,
To be one day invisible?—Earth! Invisible!
What task do you press on us, if not transformation?[8]

This yearning within nature for a new relationship with spirit is what Jung struggled to express in his theological writings, which always stressed, using alchemical and gnostic models, the need for the marriage of spirit and nature in a new, supraordinate unity. The obvious challenge that such 'androgynous' or gnostic directions hold for Western culture in general, and for Christianity in particular, is the subject of several of his major essays, especially the memorable *Answer to Job*.[9] The same incarnational mood and temper can be found in the works of Paul Tillich, Teilhard de Chardin, Mathew Fox, and a great many recent theologians and thinkers. I find this new religious sensibility heartening, and the cosmic scale of this new experiment gives enormous dimension and cultural meaning to the confusions and anxieties of the present.

We need go no further than our own adopted literary son, Grant Watson, to find the gnostic theory of the 'broadening process of incarnation' fully developed. In *Descent of Spirit*, Watson the polymath puts an artistic, biological and ecological case for what he calls the 'gradual incarnation of the *logos*'.[10] In Watson's view, the materialist model of reality is 'self-contained, restricted and barren',[11] and he argues that most scientific accounts of phenomena allow the essential aspect of life to escape. It is in 'the background of the unknown' that the solutions to our problems must be sought: 'independent of our subjective thinking and feeling, an objective and all-enfolding reality … is finding incarnation in this world that we perceive with our senses'.[12]

In Australian experience, spirit appeared to die but was actually forced into a descent or *nekyia* into the lower realm, where it was engaged in an incarnational movement toward nature. This movement is intangible and complex, and no single metaphor or concept can ever adequately describe or define it. In this book, several metaphors and concepts have been attempted. In Chapter 1, the descent was discussed in terms of human nature, a descent to the unconscious psyche, wherein shadow, instinct, aggression, and an anti-establishment temper were activated and aroused. From this descent, a new social order was born, an order that was natural, earthy, unsophisticated, and fiercely supportive of ordinary values and common sense. However, although squarely based on the natural man, this order was also heavily defended against aspects of feminine nature, and it lived in fear of being completely dissolved in the unconscious. Chapter 2 looked beyond human nature to nature itself. Here we noted a similar complex situation: spirit moving down into nature, but this movement was frustrated and denied by a fearful human spirit, which would not voluntarily submit to this descent. Nevertheless, the pull of nature is so strong that spirit is being dragged against its own will toward the aboriginal earth. Australian culture is a site of involuntary sacrifice to the archaic depths of chthonic nature.

Chapters 4 and 5 presented detailed literary accounts of what could be termed the frustration of archetypal intent. Lawrence felt the pull of nature in this country and was imaginatively attracted by it, but emotionally repelled and horrified, fearing the disintegration of consciousness. Patrick White's Voss responds to the archetypal imperative, but does so with utter abandon and as if in a trance, personifying in his grand act of self-destruction the unconscious compulsion toward sacrifice in the national psyche.

Chapters 6 to 9 focused on recent dramatic shifts in Australia, including the collapse of traditional barriers of defence, the weakening of cultural boundaries, and the intrusion of various kinds of otherness or foreignness into Australian consciousness. The fulfilment of the archetypal imperative, namely the engagement with deeper and 'foreign' levels of human and nonhuman nature, leads to a certain dissolution of hardened aspects of the social ego, but also leads to cultural re-enchantment and spiritual transformation. What takes place, when spirit is allowed to wed archaic nature in the way dictated to us by the *Zeitgeist*, is a spiritual reactivation and regeneration of nature, a new awareness of the living, dynamic relatedness between humanity, nature and spirit. A new 'dreaming' or animism is discovered, or rediscovered, as the natural world is mysteriously animated by the incarnational spirit which brings a new ecological cosmology into being.

This transformation, inspired by nature and the archetypal feminine, is currently on the horizon of cultural awareness. The patriarchal, heroic ego still reigns in the conscious sphere, in our political and social institutions, in the uppermost layers of human experience. But down below, beneath the cultural surface, a new era is being prepared, which is partly already anticipated by new age spirituality, feminist theology, and deep ecology. Some may laugh at or dismiss these phenomena now, but they will not be laughing for long, because when archetypes are set on achieving goals these goals will be achieved, as we have already seen, either with or without conscious cultural co-operation. It is simply that things go very much better when the culture understands what is demanded of it, when it becomes conscious of the directions in which it has to move. This awareness of being guided is very difficult to convey to many Australians, who still believe in the old rational enlightenment world-view, who imagine we are alone in a hostile or neutral universe, heroically steering our own course toward we know not what end. The archetypes, however, have other ideas, are teleologically oriented, and are currently committed to the re-emergence of the feminine in our time.

We are at the edge of a new experience of the sacred. The world itself is at this same edge, although it is currently 'on edge', fearing that the worst will happen. Since we are now at the end of a century and a millennium, it is to be expected that we become filled with millennial fear and dread, sensing some holocaust or apocalypse. There will, I think, be 'revelation' of a kind, but it will be transformative and incarnational, and will not be initiated by some wrathful God wanting retribution and world-cataclysm, but by the feminine face of God—Gaia, Sophia or the spirit of earth—wanting to be acknowledged and admitted fully into human consciousness and into theological divinity.[13] A spiritual feminism at the depths of the psyche will achieve for the earth what political feminism demands for women: increased status and overdue recognition and empowerment.

Australia is uniquely placed not only to demonstrate this world-wide experience but also to act as a guiding example to the rest of the world. Although traditionally at the edge of the world, Australia may well become the centre of attention as our transformational changes are realised in the future. Because the descent of spirit has been accelerated here by so many regional factors, and because nature here is so deep, archaic, and primordial, what will arise from this archetypal fusion may well be awesome and spectacular. In this regard, I have recently been encouraged by Max Charlesworth's essay 'Terra Australis and The Holy Spirit'. In a surprisingly direct—and unguarded?—moment, Charlesworth says: 'I have a feeling in my bones that there is a possibility of a creative religious explosion occurring early in the next millennium with the ancient land of Australia at the centre of it, and that the Holy Spirit may come home at last to *Terra Australis*'.[14] I am pleased that this has already been said, because if Charlesworth had not said it, I would have been forced to find within myself exactly the same prophetic utterance.

I would like to complete this book with a last glance at A.D. Hope's 'Australia', which is a poem I have referred to several times in the course of these chapters. The final stanzas read as follows:

> Yet there are some like me turn gladly home
> From the lush jungle of modern thought, to find
> The Arabian desert of the human mind,
> Hoping, if still from the deserts the prophets come,
>
> Such savage and scarlet as no green hills dare
> Springs in that waste, some spirit which escapes
> The learned doubt, the chatter of cultured apes
> Which is called civilization over there.[15]

The first and longest part of Hope's 'Australia' is concerned with the death-phase of our cultural experience. At the start of the poem, he presents the colonialist disappointment and disillusionment in this continent; it is 'a nation of trees, drab green and desolate grey'; it is 'the last of lands, the emptiest'. Australia, unlike America, is not promising territory for the advancement and development of the heroic spirit of progress. In fact, Australia is explicitly linked with the death of the hero and the degeneration of culture: 'In them at last the ultimate men arrive / Whose boast is not: "we live" but "we survive", / A type who will inhabit the dying earth'.

Then, after five stunning stanzas of death imagery and negativity, the rebirth of spirit is heralded. This new spirit arises from 'the Arabian desert of the human mind', indicating that Australia functions here as a mythic image for metaphysical wilderness. It is only in exile, at the edge of the known world, and in our case 'down under', that the voice of revelation and guidance is heard, as in Hope's example of Moses in Egypt. It is only while not-at-home in a geographical sense that we are summoned to fulfil our religious mission and are returned to our spiritual homeland.

The new spirit is 'savage and scarlet as no green hills dare'. After contact with archaic nature and the red earth, spirit rises again in a form that is qualitatively different from our ancestral English or European spirit. Spirit will be 'savage' in the sense of being untamed, primordial, not Wordsworthian, romantic, or consoling. 'Scarlet' suggests not only the red earth and mountain ranges, but also blood, instinct, passion. This spirit is red-blooded and will bear the blood-insignia of all those who have died to bring it to birth. The blood of Voss, Richard Mahony, and countless other literary figures; of Leichhardt, Eyre, and other explorers who lie in eternal tryst with the desert landscape; the blood of all the men and women who have made voluntary or involuntary sacrifices to Australia; and of countless indigenous people killed in undeclared civil war or slaughtered in organised massacres: their blood will be fused into the scarlet spirit that Hope saw in his finest visionary moment.

Not only the dead, but the living too will have to make enormous sacrifices before this spirit can be born. Les Murray wrote: 'sooner or later, I will have to give some blood for dancing here'.[16] Sacrifices to the *other* in whichever form we acknowledge it must be made by the living. We will have to sacrifice our pride, our arrogance, our hubris, before the old spirit can be allowed to merge with nature and revivify the natural world. The recent hysterical response of some Australians to the belated recognition of native land entitlements of the Aboriginal people suggests that as a nation we are not yet in the sacrificial mood. But spiritual progress will be made, with or without our consent. We cannot hold back indefinitely the transformation that is being thrust upon us by forces greater than the rational mind and its 'learned doubt' (A.D. Hope). We will have to *unlearn* that doubt, transcend our habitual scepticism, and learn to trust the archetypal vision that longs to be realised.

Notes

References to the writings of C.G. Jung will be indicated by the essay or chapter, followed by CW (*Collected Works*), the Volume number, and page or paragraph number. All references are to *The Collected Works of C.G. Jung*, translated by R.F.C. Hull, edited by H. Read, M. Fordham, G. Adler, and Wm. McGuire, and published in England by Routledge and Kegan Paul, London, and in America by Princeton University Press, Bollingen Series XX, 1953–1992. There are 20 volumes in the collected works, plus 4 supplementary volumes.

Page iii

1 Les Murray, 'First Essay on Interest', *The People's Otherworld*, Sydney: Angus & Robertson, 1983, p. 8.

Preface

1 Manning Clark, *A History of Australia*, Volumes I–VI, Melbourne University Press, 1962–87.

2 Of particular interest are Les Murray, *Collected Poems*, Sydney: Angus & Robertson, 1991; *Persistence in Folly*, Sydney: Sirius, 1984; *Embodiment and Incarnation*, Brisbane: Aquinas Library, 1987; also Les Murray, ed., *Anthology of Religious Australian Poetry*, Melbourne: Collins Dove, 1991.

3 Tony Kelly, *A New Imagining: Towards an Australian Spirituality*, Melbourne: Collins Dove, 1990; Veronica Brady, *Caught in the Draught*, Sydney: Angus & Robertson, 1994.

4 On the historical antagonism between gnosticism and orthodox Christianity, see Elaine Pagels, 'Whose Church Is the "True Church"?' in *The Gnostic Gospels*, New York: Random House, 1979.

5 See Andrew Samuels, 'Depth Psychology, Difference, and Nationalism', in *The Political Psyche*, London: Routledge, 1993, pp. 326–36.

6 See Peter Bishop, 'Singing the Land: Australia in Search of Its Soul', *Spring 49* (Dallas), 1989, pp. 19–36.

Epigraphs

1 Helen Garner and Michael Leunig, 'A Kind of Reality', *Art Monthly Australia*, Number 56, December–February 1992–93, p. 4.

2 James Hillman, *Re-Visioning Psychology* (1975), New York: Harper Collins, 1992, p. xvi.

3 Robert Bellah, *The Broken Covenant*, New York: Seabury, 1976, p. 162.

4 Veronica Brady, *Caught in the Draught*, Sydney: Angus & Robertson, 1994, p. 9.

5 Max Charlesworth, 'Terra Australis and the Holy Spirit', in Helen Daniel, ed., *Millennium*, Melbourne: Penguin, 1992, p. 287.

Introduction

1 Les Murray, 'The Dialectic of Dreams', in *The People's Otherworld*, Sydney: Angus & Robertson, 1983, p. 66.

2 C.G. Jung, 'Commentary on *The Secret of the Golden Flower*' (1929), *CW* 13, para. 54.

3 Andrew Samuels, 'The mirror and the hammer: The politics of resacralization', in *The Political Psyche*, London: Routledge, 1993, pp. 3–24.

4 See John Carroll, *Humanism: The Wreck of Western Culture*, London: Fontana, 1993.

5 For the best account to date of what a postmodern spirituality would look like, see David Ray Griffin, ed., *Spirituality and Society: Postmodern Visions*, Albany: State University of New York Press, 1988; also David Ray Griffin, *God and Religion in the Postmodern World*, Albany: State University of New York Press, 1989.

6 A.G. Stephens, in Leon Cantrell, ed., *A.G. Stephens: Selected Writings*, Sydney: Angus & Robertson, 1977, p. 395.

7 Mircea Eliade, *The Quest: History and Meaning in Religion* (1969), Chicago: University of Chicago Press, 1975.

8 Mircea Eliade, 'A New Humanism', in *The Quest*, ibid.

9 Judith Wright, 'The Upside-Down Hut' (1961), in John Barnes, ed., *The Writer in Australia*, Melbourne: Oxford University Press, 1969, p. 332.

10 George Johnston, quoted by Les Murray in 'Some Religious Stuff I Know About Australia', *Persistence in Folly*, p. 115.

11 W.C. Wentworth, 'Australasia' (1823), in G.A. Wilkes, ed., *The Colonial Poets*, Sydney: Angus & Robertson, 1974, p. 5.

12 Christopher Koch, *The Year of Living Dangerously*, London: Michael Joseph, 1978, p. 57.

13 Robert Johnson, *Ecstasy: Understanding the Psychology of Joy*, San Francisco: Harper & Row, 1989, p. 21.

Chapter 1

1 Randolph Stow, *To the Islands* (1958), Melbourne: Penguin, 1978, p. 208.

2 See A.P. Elkin, *The Australian Aborigines*, Sydney: Angus & Robertson, 1974.

3 James McAuley, 'Envoi', in Leonie Kramer, ed., *James McAuley*, Brisbane: University of Queensland Press, 1988, p. 65.

4 A.D. Hope, 'Australia', *Collected Poems 1930–1970*, Sydney: Angus & Robertson, 1972.

5 See Suzanne Falkiner, 'To the Inland Sea' and 'The Inland of the Imagination' in her *Wilderness: The Writer's Landscape*, Sydney: Simon & Schuster, 1992.

6 Martin Boyd, *The Cardboard Crown*, London: The Cresset Press, 1952.

7 See Billy Marshall-Stoneking, *Lasseter, The Making of a Legend*, Sydney: Allen & Unwin, 1985.

8 D.W. Harding, *The Hierarchy of Heaven and Earth* (1952), Gainesville: University of Florida Press, 1979.

9 Mark Twain, 'More Tramps Abroad' (1897), reprinted in *Mark Twain in Australia and New Zealand*, Melbourne: Penguin, 1973.

10 I am indebted to Susan Dwyer for this idea.

11 I have already attempted to argue this in a number of places, especially in 'The absent father' in my *Patrick White: Fiction and the Unconscious*, Melbourne: Oxford University Press, 1988.

12 In a letter to me, Gerald Murnane expressed reservations about my continued characterisation of the Australian earth as feminine-maternal. In Aboriginal myths the earth is maternal, in pagan European myths the situation is the same; and in my dreams and fantasies the earth is mother. I cannot divorce myself from this archetypal background.

13 Les Murray, 'Some Religious Stuff I Know About Australia', p. 116.

14 Randolph Stow, 'Raw Material' (1961), reprinted in Leonie Kramer and Adrian Mitchell, eds, *The Oxford Anthology of Australian Literature*, Melbourne: Oxford University Press, 1985, p. 314.

15 Vincent Buckley, 'Imagination's Home', in A. Clark, J. Fletcher and R. Marsden, eds, *Between Two Worlds: 'Loss of Faith' and Late Nineteenth Century Australian Literature*, Sydney: Wentworth Books, 1979.

16 Paul Eluard, 'Saisons', in Marilyn Kallet, trans., *Last Love Poems of Paul Eluard*, Baton Rouge: Louisiana State University Press, 1980, p. 25.

17 Peter O'Connor discusses this at length in his *Dreams and the Search for Meaning*, Sydney: Methuen Haynes, 1986.

Chapter 2

1 Bruce Chatwin, *The Songlines*, London: Picador, 1987, p. 6.

2 Leon and Rebeca Grinberg, *Psychoanalytic Perspectives on Migration and Exile* (1984), New Haven: Yale University Press, 1989.

3 Grinberg, ibid., p. 74.

4 This problem is sensitively explored in Catherine Helen Spence's colonial novel, *Clara Morison* (1854), ed. S. Magarey, Adelaide: Wakefield Press, 1986.

5 Joseph Furphy, *Such is Life* (1903), ed. J. Barnes, Brisbane: University of Queensland Press, 1981; for a good selection of Henry Lawson's short fiction see *Henry Lawson*, ed. B. Kiernan, Brisbane: University of Queensland Press, 1976.

6 Russel Ward, *The Australian Legend* (1958), revised edition, Melbourne: Oxford University Press, 1970.

7 See Jung, 'The Shadow' (1951), in CW 9, part ii.

8 Robert A. Johnson, *Owning Your Own Shadow: Understanding the Dark Side of the Psyche*, San Francisco: Harper Collins, 1993, pp. 42–7.

9 James Hillman, *Re-Visioning Psychology* (1975), New York: Harper Collins, 1992, p. 225.

10 Robert Hughes has suggestively explored this metaphor in 'The Geographical Unconscious' in *The Fatal Shore*, London: Pan, 1987.

11 Douglas Stewart, *Ned Kelly* (1943), in Alrene Sykes, ed., *Three Australian Plays*, Melbourne: Penguin, 1985.

12 W.K. Hancock, *Australia*, London: Benn, 1930, p. 284.

13 Colin Roderick, *Henry Lawson: A Life*, Sydney: Angus & Robertson, 1991.

14 Barbara Baynton, *Bush Studies* (1902), Sydney: Angus & Robertson, 1989.

15 Douglas Stewart, *Ned Kelly*, op. cit.; Sidney Nolan and Robert Melville, *Ned Kelly: 27 Paintings by Sidney Nolan*, London: Thames & Hudson, 1964; Robert Drewe, *Our Sunshine*, Sydney: Pan Macmillan, 1991.

16 D.H. Lawrence, *Kangaroo* (1923), The Corrected Edition, Sydney: Angus & Robertson, 1992, p. 18.

17 Lawrence, ibid., p. 321.

18 C.G. Jung, 'The Complications of American Psychology' (1930), *CW* 10, p. 506.

19 Jung, ibid., pp. 505–6.

20 Lawrence, p. 24.

21 Lawrence, p. 324.

22 Lawrence, p. 24.

23 Lawrence, p. 326.

24 Erich Neumann, *The Origins and History of Consciousness* (1949), Princeton University Press, 1973.

25 This aspect of modern society is memorably expressed in A.D. Hope's poem 'Standardisation' (1955) in his *Selected Poems*, Sydney: Angus & Robertson, 1992, p. 31.

26 Jung, ibid., p. 506.

27 William Blake, 'The Marriage of Heaven and Hell' (1793), in Alfred Kazin, ed., *The Portable Blake*, New York: Viking, 1975, p. 258.

28 See Terry Colling, *Beyond Mateship: Understanding Australian Men*, Sydney: Simon & Schuster, 1992.

29 See David Tacey, 'Reconstructing Masculinity', *Meanjin* (Melbourne), Vol. 49, No. 4, Summer 1990, pp. 781–94.

30 Furphy, op. cit., Eve Langley, *The Pea-Pickers* (1942), Sydney: Angus & Robertson, 1991.

31 Alfred Adler, *The Individual Psychology of Alfred Adler*, New York: Basic Books, 1964.

32 Henry Kingsley, *The Recollections of Geoffry Hamlyn* (1859), Melbourne: Lloyd O'Neil, 1970.

33 S. Freud, *New Introductory Lectures on Psycho-Analysis* (1930), Standard Edition, Vol. 22, London, Hogarth Press, 1974, p. 80.

34 For all references to A.B. Paterson's poems, see *The Collected Verse of A.B. Paterson*, Sydney: Angus & Robertson, 1982.

35 Lawson, in Kiernan, ed., p. 130.

36 Furphy, in Barnes, ed., p. 66.

37 W.C. Wentworth, 'Australasia' (1823), in G.A. Wilkes, ed., *The Colonial Poets*, Sydney: Angus & Robertson, 1974, p. 5.

38 W.C. Wentworth, in G.A. Wilkes, *The Stockyard and the Croquet Lawn*, Melbourne: Arnold, 1981, p. 15.

39 A.G. Stephens (1899), in Leon Cantrell, ed., *A.G. Stephens: Selected Writings*, Sydney: Angus & Robertson, p. 394.

Chapter 3

1 Barcroft Boake, 'Where the Dead Men Lie' (1897), in John Barnes and Brian McFarlane, eds, *Cross-Country: A Book of Australian Verse*, Melbourne: Heinemann, 1984, p. 225.

2 Henry Handel Richardson, *Australia Felix* (1917), in *The Fortunes of Richard Mahony* (1917–29), Melbourne: Penguin, 1982, p. 13.

3 D.H. Lawrence, *Kangaroo*, p. 8.

4 Patrick White, *Happy Valley*, London: Harrap, 1939, p. 28.

5 A.D. Hope, 'Australia' (1939), *Collected Poems 1930–1970*, Sydney: Angus & Robertson, p. 13.

6 Henry Handel Richardson, p. 7.

7 Patrick White, *Voss* (1957), Melbourne: Penguin, 1960.

8 Randolph Stow, 'The Singing Bones' (1966), in A. J. Hassall, ed., *Randolph Stow*, Brisbane: University of Queensland Press, 1990, p. 207.

9 Judith Wright, 'The Upside Down Hut' (1961), in John Barnes, ed., *The Writer in Australia*, Melbourne: Oxford University Press, 1969, p. 335.

10 Joan Lindsay, *Picnic at Hanging Rock* (1967), Melbourne: Penguin, 1970.

11 *Picnic at Hanging Rock*, directed by Peter Weir, produced by Hal and Jim McElroy, South Australian Film Corporation, 1975.

12 See for example John Bryson, *Evil Angels*, Melbourne: Penguin, 1985.

13 *Evil Angels*, directed by Fred Schepisi, produced by Verity Lambert, Warner Brothers, 1988.

14 Judith Wright, 'At Cooloolah' (1955), *A Human Pattern: Selected Poems*, Sydney: Angus and Robertson, 1990, p. 83.

15 Andrew Taylor, *Reading Australian Poetry*, Brisbane: University of Queensland Press, 1987, p. 35.

16 Judith Wright, 'Eroded Hills' (1953), *A Human Pattern*, p. 49.

17 C.G. Jung, 'Mind and Earth' (1927/1931), CW 10, p. 49.

18 Judith Wright, 'Bullocky' (1946), *A Human Pattern*, p. 9.

19 Bruce Chatwin, *The Songlines*, London: Picador, 1987, pp. 13–14.

Chapter 4

1 D.H. Lawrence, *Kangaroo* (1923), The Corrected Edition, Sydney: Angus & Robertson, 1992, p. 8. All references within the text are to this edition.

2 See for instance A.D. Hope, 'D.H. Lawrence's *Kangaroo*: How It Looks To An Australian', in W.S. Ramson, ed., *The Australian Experience*, Canberra: Australian National University Press, 1974.

3 D.H. Lawrence, *The Boy in the Bush* (with Mollie Skinner), (1924), Paul Eggert, ed., Cambridge: Cambridge University Press, 1990. All references are to this edition.

4 See bibliographical reference in note 13.

5 Randolph Stow, 'The Singing Bones', in *Randolph Stow*, ed. Anthony J. Hassall, Brisbane: University of Queensland Press, 1990, p. 207.

6 A.D. Hope, 'Australia'.

7 Randolph Stow makes this same point in his 'Raw Material' (1961), in L. Kramer and A. Mitchell, eds, *The Oxford Anthology of Australian Literature*, Melbourne: Oxford University Press, 1985, p. 314.

8 See note 13.

9 D.H. Lawrence, *Fantasia of the Unconscious* (1923), Harmondsworth: Penguin, 1971.

10 D.H. Lawrence, *Studies in Classic American Literature* (1923), Harmondsworth: Penguin, 1971, p. 145.

11 Ronald Conway, *The Great Australian Stupor*, second edition, Melbourne: Sun Books, 1985.

12 Jung, 'The Relations between the Ego and the Unconscious' (1928), *CW* 7; and also 'Conscious, Unconscious, and Individuation' (1939), *CW* 9, part 1.

13 D.H. Lawrence, 'Letter to Katharine Throssell' (1922), in *The Letters of D.H. Lawrence, Vol. IV*, (letter 2550), ed. Roberts et al., Cambridge University Press, 1987.

Chapter 5

1 See Marie-Louise von Franz, *An Introduction to the Psychology of Fairy Tales* (1970), Dallas: Spring Publications, 1978.

2 Most critical writing about *Voss* views the central figure in an heroic or progressive light. See for instance G.A. Wilkes, ed., *Ten Essays on Patrick White*, Sydney: Angus and Robertson, 1970, and Patricia Morley, *The Mystery of Unity*, Brisbane: University of Queensland Press, 1972.

3 H.P. Heseltine, in his Introduction and Notes to Patrick White's *Voss* (1957), Sydney: Longman, 1965, pp. 389–90.

4 Patrick White, *Voss* (1957), Melbourne: Penguin, 1990, p. 69. All references are to this edition.

5 Jung, 'Concerning Archetypes, with Special Reference to the Anima Concept' (1936/1954) *CW* 9, part 1.

6 In Jungian terms, Voss's life follows the pattern of the *puer aeternus*, the 'eternal boy' who remains infantile and self–destructive because of a primal attachment to the mother. See Jung, *Symbols of Transformation*, *CW* 5, and Marie-Louise von Franz, *Puer Aeternus* (1970), Santa Monica: Sigo Press, 1981.

7   Jung, 'Approaching the Unconscious', in *Man and His Symbols*, New York: Doubleday, 1964, pp. 18–103.

8   See my book, *Patrick White: Fiction and the Unconscious*, Melbourne: Oxford University Press, 1988.

9   This is fully discussed in Erich Neumann, 'The Ego Germ in the Original Uroboric Situation', *The Origins and History of Consciousness* (1949), Princeton University Press, 1973.

10 See E.O. James, *The Cult of the Mother Goddess*, London: Thames and Hudson, 1959.

11 See J.G. Frazer, 'The Myth and Ritual of Attis', in *The Golden Bough*, Part IV, Vol. I, *Adonis, Attis, Osiris* (1906), London: Macmillan, 1976.

12 Jung, 'On the Psychology of the Unconscious' (1917/1943), *CW* 7.

Chapter 6

1   Mircea Eliade, *The Sacred and the Profane*, New York: Harcourt, Brace, 1959, p. 9.

2   John Carroll, 'The Australian Way of Life', in J. Carroll, ed., *Intruders in the Bush*, Second Edition, Melbourne: Oxford University Press, 1992, p. 234.

3   Les Murray, 'Some Religious Stuff I Know About Australia', p. 116.

4   Arthur Rimbaud, in Wallace Fowlie, ed., *Rimbaud: Complete Works, Selected Letters*, University of Chicago Press, 1966, p. 305.

5   See for instance Ken Gelder and Paul Salzman, *The New Diversity*, Melbourne: McPhee Gribble, 1989.

6   See for instance Elizabeth Jolley, *Mr Scobie's Riddle*, Melbourne: Penguin, 1983; and *The Well*, Melbourne: Penguin, 1986.

7   Helen Garner, *Cosmo Cosmolino*, Melbourne: McPhee Gribble, 1992.

8   Tim Winton, *That Eye, The Sky*, Melbourne: Penguin, 1986; and *Cloudstreet*, Melbourne: Penguin, 1991.

9   Gerald Murnane, *Landscape with Landscape*, Melbourne: Penguin, 1987; and *Inland*, Melbourne: Heinemann, 1988.

10 Gerald Murnane, *The Plains*, Melbourne: Penguin, 1984, p. 37: 'And according to the projections of real, that is spiritual geography, the plains clearly did not coincide with any pretended land of Australia.'

11 See Chapter 5 and the Conclusion of my book *Patrick White: Fiction and the Unconscious*.

12 Michael Leunig and Helen Garner, 'A Kind of Reality', *Art Monthly Australia*, Number 56, Summer Issue, December– February 1992–3, p. 4.

Chapter 7

1 See L.R. Hiatt, ed., *Australian Aboriginal Mythology*, Canberra: Australian Institute of Aboriginal Studies, 1975, and Margaret King-Boyes, 'Creation and Cosmology: Man and Nature' in *Patterns of Aboriginal Culture: Then and Now*, Sydney: McGraw Hill, 1977.

2 A.A. Phillips, *The Australian Tradition*, second edition, Melbourne: Cheshire-Lansdowne, 1966.

3 Les Murray, 'The Inverse Transports', in *Dog Fox Field*, Sydney: Angus & Robertson, 1990, pp. 20–1.

4 W.E.H. Stanner, *White Man Got No Dreaming: Essays 1938–1973*, Canberra: Australian National University Press, 1979.

5 See Bob Hodge and Vijay Mishra, *Dark Side of the Dream: Australian Literature and the Postcolonial Mind*, Sydney: Allen & Unwin, 1991.

6 Jung, *Psychology and Alchemy* (1944), CW 12, 1953/1968, para. 126.

7 Jung, 'Mind and Earth' (1927/1931), CW 10, p. 49.

8 See Brian Elliott, *The Jindyworobaks*, Brisbane: University of Queensland Press, 1979.

9 Malidoma Some, *Ritual: Power, Healing, and Community*, Portland: Swan Raven, 1993, p. 34.

10 Oodgeroo of the tribe Noonuccal (formerly Kath Walker), 'We are Going', in J. Tranter and P. Mead, eds, *The Penguin Book of Modern Australian Poetry*, Melbourne: Penguin, 1991, p. 103.

11 Interesting reflections on this theme can be found in Robert L. Gardner, *The Rainbow Serpent: Bridge to Consciousness*, Toronto: Inner City Books, 1990. On page 9 we read: 'White and black mentalities in Australia [are] mirror versions of each other. What is accepted by one is rejected by the other ... Each community represents the unknown or shadow side that is repressed by the other'.

12 See Tony Swain, *Interpreting Aboriginal Religion: An Historical Account*, Adelaide: Australian Association for the Study of Religions, 1985.

13 The key role of an Earth Mother (such as Kunapipi) in the religion and mythology of Aboriginal society is widely supported in the literature, as is evident in the works of Hiatt, King-Boyes, Stanner, Swain, Elkin, and others.

14 Erich Neumann, 'The Great Mother', in *The Origins and History of Consciousness* (1949), Princeton University Press, 1973. Some may find this analysis of Aboriginal culture Euro-centric, but the claim of Jungian psychology, which I support, is that archetypal processes such as those described here are found in all cultures and at all times in world history, by virtue of a collective dimension in the human psyche.

15 See Erich Neumann, 'The Ego Germ in the Original Uroboric Situation', in *Origins*.

16 E.O. James, *The Cult of the Mother Goddess*, London: Thames & Hudson, 1959.

17 See Jack Davis, Stephen Muecke, et al., eds, *Paperbark: A Collection of Black Australian Writings*, Brisbane: University of Queensland Press, 1990; and also Kevin Gilbert, ed., *Inside Black Australia: An Anthology of Aboriginal Poetry*, Melbourne: Penguin, 1988.

18 Mudrooroo Narogin, *Writing from the Fringe: A Study of Modern Aboriginal Literature*, Melbourne: Hyland House, 1990, p. 171. On the same page he speaks of the 'simple binary opposition of the white-evil opposed to the black-good'.

19 Jung, in a letter to Bill W., January 30, 1961, quoted in Jan Bauer, *Alcoholism and Women: The Background and the Psychology*, Toronto: Inner City Books, 1982, p. 127. Jung's ideas on alcoholism are also discussed in Lewis Hyde, *Alcohol and Poetry: The Booze Talking*, Dallas: The Dallas Institute Publications, 1986.

20 See Mudrooroo Narogin, *Wild Cat Falling* (1965), Sydney: Angus & Robertson, 1979; *Long Live Sandawara*, Melbourne: Quartet, 1979; and *The Song Circle of Jacky and Selected Poems*, Melbourne: Hyland House, 1986.

21 Mudrooroo Narogin, *Master of the Ghost Dreaming*, Sydney: Angus & Robertson, 1991, pp. 1–2.

22 Oodgeroo Noonuccal, 'The Past', in *Inside Black Australia*, p. 99. On page 95, Oodgeroo writes: 'Do not ask of us / To be deserters, to disown our mother, / To change the unchangeable'.

Chapter 8

1 Grant Watson, in Dorothy Green, ed., *Descent of Spirit: Writings of E.L. Grant Watson*, Sydney: Primavera Press, 1990, p. 119.

2 See Margaret King-Boyes, *Patterns of Aboriginal Culture*, Sydney: McGraw-Hill, 1977.

3 Judith Wright, 'Landscape and Dreaming' in Stephen R. Graubard, ed., *Australia: The Daedalus Symposium*, Sydney: Angus & Robertson, 1985, p. 32.

4 S. Freud, *The Psychopathology of Everyday Life* (1901), *The Standard Edition of the Complete Psychological Works*, Vol. 6, London: The Hogarth Press, 1953, pp. 258–9.

5 See Richard White, *Inventing Australia*, Sydney: Allen & Unwin, 1981.

6 Judith Wright, 'Bora Ring' (1946), *A Human Pattern*, Sydney: Angus & Robertson, 1990, p. 2.

7 Annie Dillard, *Teaching a Stone to Talk*, London: Picador, 1984, p. 70.

8 These issues are explored by Peter Bishop in 'Facing the World: Depth Psychology and Deep Ecology', *Harvest* (London), Vol. 36, pp. 62–71, and also in his *The Greening of Psychology*, Dallas: Spring Publications, 1990.

9 Oodgeroo Noonuccal, 'The Unhappy Race', in Kevin Gilbert, *Inside Black Australia*, Melbourne: Penguin, 1988, p. 98.

10 Levy-Bruhl, *Primitive Mythology: The Mythic World of the Australian and Papuan Natives*, trans. Brian Elliott, Brisbane: University of Queensland Press, 1983.

11 D.H. Lawrence, 'Herman Melville's *Typee* and *Omoo*', in *Studies in Classic American Literature* (1923), Harmondsworth: Penguin, 1977, pp. 144–6.

12 David Ray Griffin and Huston Smith, *Primordial Truth and Postmodern Theology*, Albany: State University of New York Press, 1989; and Matthew Fox, *Creation Spirituality*, San Francisco: HarperCollins, 1991.

13 Rupert Sheldrake, *The Rebirth of Nature: The Greening of Science and God*, New York: Bantam, 1991.

14 William Irwin Thompson, *At the Edge of History*, Great Barrington, Mass.: Lindisfarne Press, 1990.

15 Christopher Bamford, *Ecology and Holiness*, Great Barrington, Mass.: Lindisfarne Press, 1982.

16 William Irwin Thompson and David Spangler, *The Reimagination of the World*, Santa Fe: Bear & Co., 1991.

17 Jung, 'Transformation Symbolism in the Mass' (1942/1954), CW 11, p. 245.

18 Jung, 'The State of Psychotherapy Today' (1934), CW 10, para. 367.

19 Jung, in Gerhard Adler, ed., *C.G. Jung: Letters*, Vol. 1, Princeton University Press, 1989, p. 338.

20 Jung, *Psychological Types* (1921), CW 6, p. 630.

21 Jung, 'On the Nature of the Psyche' (1947/1954), CW 8, p. 215.

22 James Hillman, '*Anima Mundi*: The Return of the Soul to the World', *Spring 1982* (Dallas), pp. 71–93; also published in his *The Thought of the Heart and the Soul of the World*, Dallas: Spring Publications, 1992.

23 James Hillman and Michael Ventura, *We've Had a Hundred Years of Psychotherapy and the World's Getting Worse*, San Francisco: HarperCollins, 1992.

24 For the various sources that have contributed to Hillman's thinking about imaginal reality, see Hillman, *Archetypal Psychology: A Brief Account*, Dallas: Spring Publications, 1983.

25 James Hillman, 'Dehumanizing or Soul-making', *Re-Visioning Psychology* (1975), second edition, New York: HarperCollins, 1992, p. 173.

26 These works are too numerous to cite here; see various works by Edward S. Casey, Paul Kugler, Robert Romanyshyn, Alfred Ziegler, Wolfgang Giegerich, Peter Bishop, Michael Vannoy Adams, Robert Sardello.

27 See Roberts Avens, 'Soul and World', in *The New Gnosis: Heidegger, Hillman, and Angels*, Dallas: Spring Publications, 1984.

28 As discussed in Chapter 1 of this book.

29 See for instance Michael Leunig, *A Common Prayer*, Melbourne: Collins Dove, 1990; *A Common Philosophy*, Melbourne: David Lovell, 1992; *Everyday Devils and Angels*, Melbourne: Penguin, 1992.

30 There are important exceptions to this anti-spiritual approach to the poetry, most notably in Shirley Walker on Wright and Cliff Hanna on Neilson; see Shirley Walker, *Flame and Shadow: A Study of Judith Wright's Poetry*, Brisbane: University of Queensland Press, 1991, and Cliff Hanna, *The Folly of Spring: A Study of John Shaw Neilson's Poetry*, Brisbane: University of Queensland Press, 1990.

31 John Shaw Neilson, 'The Orange Tree' (1919), in Cliff Hanna, ed., *John Shaw Neilson*, Brisbane: University of Queensland Press, 1991, p. 82.

32 For this and the other poems mentioned by Wright, see Judith Wright, *Collected Poems*, Sydney: Angus & Robertson, 1971.

33 Les Murray, 'Noonday Axeman' (1965), *Collected Poems*, Sydney: Angus & Robertson, 1991, pp. 2–4.

34 Rodney Hall, *The Second Bridegroom*, Melbourne: McPhee Gribble, 1991, pp. 193–4. All future page references are to this edition.

35 Les Murray, 'The Human-Hair Thread' in *Persistence in Folly*, Sydney: Sirius, 1984, p. 27.

Chapter 9

1 Mircea Eliade, 'Initiation and the Modern World', in *The Quest*, p. 126.

2 Christopher Koch, *The Year of Living Dangerously*, London: Michael Joseph, 1978, p. 236.

3 Jung, 'Commentary on *The Secret of the Golden Flower*' (1929), CW 13, para. 54.

4 Patrick White, *The Solid Mandala* (1966), Melbourne: Penguin Books, 1977, p. 145.

5 Mircea Eliade, *The Sacred and the Profane* (1957), New York: Harcourt, Brace & World, 1977, p. 204.

6 This argument is forcefully expressed in John Carroll, *Humanism: The Wreck of Western Culture*, London: Fontana, 1993.

7 Camille Paglia, *Sexual Personae*, London: Penguin, 1990, p. 39.

8 Joseph Henderson, 'Ancient Myths and Modern Man', in C.G. Jung, ed., *Man and His Symbols*, New York: Doubleday, 1964.

9 An excellent work on this subject is Edward C. Whitmont, *Return of the Goddess*, New York: Crossroad, 1982.

10 See Edward Edinger, *The Creation of Consciousness*, Toronto: Inner City Books, 1984.

11 In my thinking on these matters I have been greatly influenced by feminist theology, especially these works: Mary Daly, *Beyond God the Father*, Boston: Beacon Press, 1973; Mary Daly, *Gyn/Ecology*, Boston: Beacon Press, 1978; Rosemary Reuther, *Sexism and God-Talk*, Boston: Beacon Press, 1983; Joan Chamberlain Engelsman, *The Feminine Dimension of the Divine*, Philadelphia: The Westminster Press, 1979.

12 Patrick White, *The Vivisector*, London: Cape, 1970, p. 612.

13 W.B. Yeats, 'The Second Coming' (1920), *W.B. Yeats, Selected Poetry*, Harmonsdworth: Penguin, 1991, p. 124.

14 W.B. Yeats, in the introduction to his play *The Resurrection* (1935), quoted in A.W. Allison, ed., *The Norton Anthology of Poetry*, New York: W.W. Norton, 1983, p. 883.

15 See David Miller, *The New Polytheism*, Dallas: Spring Publications, 1981.

16 Yeats, in Allison, ed., *The Norton Anthology of Poetry*, New York: W.W. Norton, 1983, p. 883.

Chapter 10

1 For a suggestive study of the 'edge' motif in Australian writing, see Martin Leer, 'At the Edge: Geography and the Imagination in the Work of David Malouf', *Australian Literary Studies*, Vol. 12, No. 1, May 1985, pp. 3–21.

2 Charles Harpur, 'The Dream by the Fountain', in Michael Ackland, ed., *Charles Harpur: Selected Poetry and Prose*, Melbourne: Penguin, 1986, p. 11.

3 Chris Wallace-Crabbe, 'Melbourne', in John Barnes and Brian McFarlane, eds, *Cross-Country: A Book of Australian Verse*, Melbourne: Heinemann, 1984, p. 261.

4 John Carroll, *Humanism*, p. 1.

5 Samuel Beckett, *Endgame* (1958), London: Faber, 1982, p. 17.

6 Elaine Pagels, *The Gnostic Gospels*, New York: Random House, 1979.

7   These gnostic theories are critically reviewed in James McAuley's essays
    'The Grinning Mirror' and 'Journey into Egypt' in Leonie Kramer, ed.,
    James McAuley, University of Queensland Press, 1988.

8   Rainer Maria Rilke, *Duino Elegies*, trans. J.B. Leishman and Stephen
    Spender, London: The Hogarth Press, 1939.

9   C.G. Jung, *Answer to Job* (1952), *Collected Works* Vol. 11.

10 Grant Watson, in Dorothy Green, ed., *Descent of Spirit: Writings of
    E.L. Grant Watson*, Sydney: Primavera Press, 1990, p. 20.

11 Watson, op. cit., p. 87.

12 Watson, op. cit., p. 233.

13 This idea is discussed at length in Edward C. Whitmont, *Return of the
    Goddess*, New York: Crossroad, 1982.

14 Max Charlesworth, '2000 A.D.: Terra Australis and the Holy Spirit' in
    Helen Daniel, ed., *Millennium: Time-Pieces by Australian Writers*,
    Melbourne: Penguin, 1991, p. 287.

15 A.D. Hope, 'Australia' (1960), *Selected Poems*, Sydney: Angus &
    Robertson, 1992, pp. 71–2.

16 Les Murray, 'The Human-Hair Thread' in *Persistence in Folly*, Sydney:
    Sirius, 1984, p. 30.

Index